JASMINE
IN HER HAIR

CULTURE AND CUISINE FROM PAKISTAN

BY HUMA SIDDIQUI

WHITE JASMINE PRESS

Cover Design and Image: Janus van Helferten - www.van-cols.co.uk
Food Photography: Michael Anthony Messner- www.bigscreendreams.com
Steve Tesmer - www.thetallguy.com
Jena Olson
Editors: Sabah Karimi
Samir Karimi
Tess Meuer
Book Design and Typesetting: Paul King
Production Manager: Janet Pulvermacher

Publisher:
White Jasmine Press, Inc.
P. O. Box 2561
Madison, WI   53701-2561

Printed in the United States of America

www.whitejasmine.com
www.curryandcorriander.com

ACKNOWLEDGEMENTS

Writing *Jasmine in Her Hair* has been an emotional, exciting and memorable journey.

I truly believe that there is not enough space to thank all the people in my life who have supported me through this journey.

My deepest gratitude goes to my loving parents. My dad Ekram Siddiqui, for teaching me to always speak my mind, explore the possibilities and move forward thoughtfully in life. My mom Iffat Siddiqui, for her lessons of perseverance and strength to combat life's challenges with grace and elegance.

My heartfelt thanks go to my children Sabah Karimi and Samir Karimi for writing the beautiful afterword and foreword for the book, their support and words of encouragement. I truly appreciate my son Samir's compassion, endless hours of editing and discussions about the book ideas.

I am thankful to my brothers Sohail Siddiqui and Nadeem Siddiqui for their tremendous encouragement and affection.

I am indebted to my delightful friends and scarf sisters, Tess Meuer and Gail Huelsing for their continuous support, numerous laughs and above all for truly believing in me. I appreciate the kindness, support and enthusiasm of all of my friends during this process.

My thanks to the publishing team Janet Pulvermacher and Paul King, for taking the project on and working through it with outstanding tenacity.

CONTENTS

FOREWORD

"Life is like an ocean. It is constantly changing and always in motion." This quote is one of the main things I remember my mom telling me when I was younger. It means that like an ocean, life itself is always changing, because it has to. She told me that if an ocean sat still for too long, then it turns into an unattractive swamp. But with the constant change in the tides, the ocean will always be fresh and beautiful. I tend to think about this quote whenever my life throws me a challenge. I really feel like I have been able to overcome a lot of difficulties and challenges in my life because of the wisdom my mother gave me.

Due to all the benefits that I have received from my wise, little mother, I really believe that having a family and a structure is essential for guidance in your own personal life. Although, I don't mean having the typical family of a mom, a dad, and 2.5 children, I mean a family of people that you love and care for. In my own life I never really had too much of a connection with my dad, as I only lived with my mom and sister.

But even though I never had that typical, complete family, I really began to understand the difference in what my mother referred to as a house to a home. Of course, there are always age-old sayings like, *home is where the heart is*, but more importantly I discovered that you could have a place to live, and consider it a mere house. Within a regular house, once it is filled with love and family, you can begin to consider it a home.

Although it may sound strange, one of the most memorable things in my home was that of my mother's cooking. After coming back from a hard day of work or school, finding the aroma of a freshly cooked chicken or beef dish, was very satisfying. It just made me feel at home, a place where the outside world stops, a little untouchable cave in a sense.

It may just be food, but I believe that it was the system that we had that made it so worthwhile. I have been noticing more and more that as I am busier with college and job, my meals are just on the go. I can eat breakfast in my car, lunch at work, and dinner quickly by the television before going to bed. A system like that is all right for a couple of days, but after a while I almost felt deprived. I had no idea that eating a home cooked meal at the dining table with my family would change my lifestyle so drastically. I believe that even if you don't have time to cook an authentic Pakistani dish, it is essential to eat whatever food is made as a family, conversing about your day and life at the table. I guess it is only one of those things that you really need.

I personally am really glad to see this book, *Jasmine in Her Hair*. I believe that it is not only filled with the recipes that I grew up with, but it is filled with my mother's spirit of cooking. As this book is a tribute to her mother, perhaps in a sense this foreword can be a tribute to mine.

To a woman who has filled
my life with love and happiness,
I will never forget my mother!

Samir Karimi
Son of Huma Siddiqui

SECTION ONE

Home Sweet Home

Graceful hills, valleys and rivers divide the beautiful country of Pakistan into four major provinces. This immensely diverse country is approximately the size of the entire state of Wisconsin and half of Illinois. Within the four provinces are five major languages: Punjabi, Baluchi, Pushto, Sindhi, and Urdu. Urdu (oor-do) is a rich language full of beauty, grace, charm, and elegance. It is the official language of Pakistan, and is in fact a modified form of the Arabic alphabet. The script is written from right to left.

The history of Urdu language lends itself to Hindi influences; Iranians who spoke Persian settled in India during the slave dynasty and brought their language with them. England conquered India and English words became part of the Urdu language; now the language is a mixture of Hindi, Persian, Arabic, and English. My name, Huma, is Persian in origin. My father used to love to explain the meaning of my name. According to him, Huma is a rare, exotic bird, which brings luck and riches to whomever she chooses. I fondly remember his description.

Growing up, a lot of emphasis was placed on learning to speak clearly. Language is an important means of communication, a way to express yourself, and reflects class. It is not about saying things, they are not only words but are rather a reflection of one's thought process. Choice of words is the key; swearing or rude words are usually not a part of the conversation even under dire circumstances. From teens to adults, I think it is a shame, how swear words and just plain rudeness have become a part of day-to-day communication. I feel it is certainly a decline in literary and intellectual standards. After ruling

People who migrated from India to Pakistan were called the Muhajirs, **which means** immigrants.

the sub-continent for two hundred years, the English left in 1947 and the sub-continent became what is now known as, India, Pakistan and Bangladesh. People who migrated from India to Pakistan were called the *Muhajirs*, which means *immigrants. Muhajirs* spoke Urdu and brought it to Pakistan with them. Respect for elders is a big part of the culture and is clearly reflected in the language. In English everyone is referred to as you. In Urdu, there are different terms to address older and younger people, for example, *aap* is used to respectfully address an older person and *tumm* is used for someone younger than yourself.

Food

Food is an extremely important part of most cultures. Dinner time is usually the time for families to talk about the day, relax and share thoughts. In Pakistan, typically the family gathers around freshly prepared spicy, aromatic food and takes the time to enjoy each other's company. There are certain foods that will remain in our memories and hearts forever, even after the people who made them, have left this world. I have lots of wonderful memories related to food. When I am having a gray day, feeling a little homesick and looking for comfort, it is really interesting that I find myself craving particular foods. Comfort food for me includes, a two egg omelet with chopped tomatoes and chili powder served with rice, or potato pakoras, which are sliced potatoes dipped in spicy gram flour batter and deep fried. Either one of these things usually does the trick. It is important to recognize the connection and treasure it, so the memories live on.

> *The legacy of food gets passed on from generation to generation, as a beautiful gift.*

The legacy of food gets passed on from generation to generation, as a beautiful gift. When I start getting special requests for certain foods from my kids then I know that they are going through stressful and challenging times. It is interesting for me as a mother to see that developing in my children. They might not recognize this secret fully at the moment but the process has started and they are gathering their treasure of memories.

Home represents a family and their values. In an Asian culture, home is usually a woman's territory and a lot of work goes into creating a comfortable and rich home for the family and friends. It is somewhere where people feel safe and relaxed, away from the rest of the world. By a rich home, I don't mean rich in material goods but rather an inviting and warm home. Hospitality is an important ingredient of the family structure and families go to great lengths to make sure the guests feel at home and are cared for in every way. Family and friends feel honored when someone opens the doors to their home and make sure that they reciprocate with the same warmth and hospitality. Sometimes, if we had visitors in the evening, Mom would invite them to stay for dinner out of courtesy and quickly instruct the cook to prepare a couple of extra dishes. Guests are considered a blessing and believed to bring good luck.

As a child, coming back from school, I felt at home as soon as I could smell the wonderful aromas of my mom's cooking. In winter, there would always be some kind of *halwa* being made. The main ingredients in *halwa*, a dessert, are semolina, or carrots, or split peas with tons of sugar, cream and nuts, delicious!

How can that not be comforting? I love to cook for family and friends; it is very gratifying to see everyone enjoying my cooking. The house feels warm and welcoming. Perhaps one of the reasons that I became more and more involved in cooking traditional food is because I missed home food since I left Pakistan.

Once I had children, it became my focus to ensure that I provide them with a taste of their own culture and heritage. Both of my children are grown and in college. My daughter, Sabah, moved out almost two years ago but still comes home every Sunday to visit, catch up and have a 'proper meal'. My son, Samir, plans to stay home for another year or so, although he started college this September. My children are hooked on Pakistani food and I enjoy every opportunity to tease them about it. I am sure they will always want to come home for the food, that is my trump card to keep them coming back. I think I am a wise mother, wouldn't you say? It is comforting to think that my children will, hopefully, always remember me as a good mother but definitely a good cook!

APPETIZERS

Samosas
Recipe on page 20
Photo by Steve Tesmer

Pakoras

DEEP FRIED POTATOES IN GRAM FLOUR BATTER

2 cups of gram flour
3 medium potatoes, peeled and
    sliced
½ teaspoon salt

1 teaspoon whole cumin
½ teaspoon chili powder
cooking oil to deep fry
1 cup water

Mix gram flour, water and all spices to make a batter. Peel and slice potatoes into thin slices. Add sliced potatoes to the batter. Heat oil in a frying pan. When hot, add one potato slice at a time. Turn the slice over when one side is done. Take it out and leave it on kitchen towel so excess oil is absorbed. Transfer to the serving dish and serve warm with yogurt or cilantro sauce.

Other vegetables, like sliced eggplant, fresh spinach,
or onions can be substituted for the potatoes.

Pua

DEEP FRIED SWEET ROUND PATTIES

1 cup plain flour
3 tablespoons semolina
1 tablespoons oil
3 tablespoons sugar
1 cup water
¼ teaspoon baking powder

½ cup sliced unsalted almonds
½ cup dried raisins
½ cup sliced unsalted pistachios
2 cups oil to fry
whipped cream

Mix all the ingredients together in a bowl, except the oil. Heat oil in a deep frying pan and spoon some of the mixture in oil and deep fry until golden brown. They are usually round and 2 inches wide. Puas are quite rich and are served warm with cream on top with hot tea.

Potato Cutlets
HARD BOILED EGGS ROLLED IN SPICY POTATOES

3 pounds red potatoes
6 hard boiled eggs
2 cups bread crumbs
½ teaspoon chili powder
½ teaspoon garam masala

½ teaspoon ground cumin
¼ teaspoon salt
2 eggs beaten
2 cups oil to fry

Boil the potatoes until soft, peel and mash the potatoes. Add all ground spices and mix thoroughly. Take a ball of mashed potato and make it into the shape of an egg. Place the egg in the middle and cover with another half of egg shaped potato ball. Dip in egg mixture and roll it in bread crumbs so it is covered on all sides. Heat oil in a frying pan and deep fry the cutlet until it is golden brown and crisp on all sides.

Samosas
DEEP FRIED PASTRY STUFFED WITH SPICY POTATOES

2 cups all-purpose flour
½ teaspoon salt
½ teaspoon kalonji (Nigella seeds)
2 tablespoon cooking oil
¼ cup warm water
½ teaspoon chili powder
½ teaspoon ground cumin
1 teaspoon whole cumin seeds

3 medium potatoes
½ teaspoon salt
1 bunch green onions, chopped
½ cup cilantro, chopped
3 cups cooking oil for frying
2 green chili peppers, chopped
   (optional)

In a medium bowl, mix flour, salt, kalonji and oil until the mixture resembles fine bread crumbs. Pour in water to make a smooth dough. Pat into a ball. Place on a lightly floured surface and knead for 10 minutes or until dough is smooth and elastic. Return to the bowl, cover and set aside.

Boil potatoes until soft, take them out of the boiling water and allow them to cool. Peel the skin and dice the potatoes into small pieces. Add all spices, green chilies, cilantro and green onions. Mix thoroughly.

Divide dough into 15 equal portions. Roll portions into balls, roll the balls into six inch circles. Cut each circle in half. Form semicircles into cones. Fill cones with equal portions of the potato mixture.

Heat oil in a large deep skillet. Carefully lower cones into preheated oil a few at a time. Fry until golden brown, 2 to 3 minutes, drain on paper towels. Serve warm with yogurt or cilantro sauce.

Samosas
Photo by Steve Tesmer

Potato Patties
Deep Fried Potato Fritters

3 pounds red potatoes
1 teaspoon chili powder
2 teaspoons salt
1 teaspoon ground cumin

1 teaspoon whole cumin
Fresh cilantro, chopped
1 egg
2 cups oil to fry

Boil the potatoes until soft, not too soft but rather more like potato salad. Take the potatoes out of the water and leave them to cool. Peel the potatoes and crush them with a fork or hand crusher. Add all the spices, cilantro, green onions and egg. Make patties and deep fry in hot oil. Serve with cilantro or yogurt side sauce.

Make sure to take the potatoes out of the water as soon as they are done. Spices mix well when potatoes are still warm.

Dahi Baras
Gram Flour Fritters in Yogurt Sauce

Fritters

2 cups gram flour
½ teaspoon chili powder
½ teaspoon ground cumin
¼ teaspoon salt

1/ teaspoon whole cumin
¼ teaspoon baking powder
1 cup water
2 cups oil to fry

Yogurt Sauce

2 cups plain yogurt
¼ cup water
¼ teaspoon chili powder

¼ teaspoon ground cumin
⅛ teaspoon salt
½ cup chopped fresh cilantro

Add gram flour, spices, baking powder and water to prepare the batter. Heat oil in a frying pan and when hot, add tablespoon of the gram flour mixture. Fry until the fritters are golden brown. Fry all the fritters and set aside.

In a bowl, mix yogurt, water and all spices. Add the fritters to the yogurt, while they are still warm. It is important because the fritters will absorb some of the yogurt while warm and remain soft. Garnish with fresh cilantro and a pinch of cumin and chili powder.

Namak Paras
DEEP FRIED SAVORY DIAMONDS

2 cups plain flour
2 tablespoons oil
1 cup warm water
½ teaspoon salt

½ teaspoon kalonji
   (Nigella seeds)
2 cups oil to fry

Add 2 tablespoons of oil, salt, kalonji and warm water to plain flour to make a dough. Roll out the dough and cut strips diagonally and then cut diagonally again in the opposite direction to make the diamonds. Heat oil in a frying pan and fry the diamonds until they turn crisp and golden. Serve with tea.

*This is a very popular dish to make ahead of time
for parties, or for tea time in the afternoons.*

Shaaker Paras
DEEP FRIED SWEET DIAMONDS

2 cups plain flour
2 tablespoons oil
½ teaspoon salt

4 tablespoons sugar
1 cup warm water
2 cups oil to fry

Add plain flour, oil, water, salt and sugar in a bowl and make a dough. Roll out the dough in a big circle and cut diagonally in strips and then diagonally again in the opposite direction, to make the diamonds. Heat oil in a deep frying pan and fry the diamonds until they are golden brown.

They are delicious when served with tea.

SECTION TWO

Day to Day Life

Cooking is a therapeutic experience for me. The colors and aroma of traditional spices in the house reminds me of home. It is quite ironic actually when I think about this. My mom was always worried about me learning to cook well. Her main concern was that because of her health problems she would not be able to teach me the traditional recipes. I wish she was alive, so she could see that all her teachings did not go to waste and I turned out to be a fairly good cook. I think me writing and publishing this book would have been a real treat for her, she would be very proud.

Pakistani cuisine recognizes the importance and characteristics of spices. A combination of different spices is called *masala*, which can vary from region to region. *Garam masala* means *hot spices* and it is a combination of five different spices: cloves; green and black cardamoms; cinnamon and cumin. All of these whole spices are roasted, powdered and stored in jars and are mainly used in meat dishes. The important thing to remember when cooking Pakistani food, is that there are some basic spices which are used in most dishes such as garlic, ginger, garam masala, chili powder, turmeric, coriander and cumin. But you can still change things to match your own mood or taste by adding less or more of each spice. It is critical to be aware of the spices as separate ingredients and what they taste like. Sometimes, eating out at an Indian or Pakistani restaurant, I feel quite frustrated when the spices are the only things I can taste. This is not considered good cooking. The spices are supposed to compliment and enhance

Pakistani cuisine recognizes the importance and characteristics of spices.

the flavor and character of the dish. I love experimenting with different spices and other ingredients, it is like being in a laboratory. I think I feel pretty safe. However, like anyone else, I have had my share of disasters when I first started cooking on my own.

Scarf Sisters

My mother made sure that I learned all the domestic chores and made a wonderful homemaker, so when I got married, my husband and in-laws would be happy with me. It is a mother's priority and pride that the daughters are taught to be good homemakers and graceful hostesses. Occasionally, I used to tease her about all this and say, *"Maybe you should look for a rich husband for me so I can hire a cook and a tailor, then all my needs would be met."* She will give me this 'look' and say, *"Yes, that is true but you still need to know how things are done so you can supervise the servants. Who wants a boss who doesn't know anything?"* It was a wise answer but I would just laugh it off. Times have changed and I am not so traditional about this issue. I would love my daughter to learn to cook the traditional food but more because I would like her to keep the family tradition alive of preparing and sharing food and to keep her family from starving.

My dad on the other hand always encouraged me to speak my mind, think things through and learn to trust my instincts and judgment. He used to say, *"Women have so much power, and it is a shame they don't use it"*. He always encouraged me to ask questions. He would always smile at my questions and say, *"You certainly are my daughter, keep asking those questions"*. I have immense gratitude for my father and I do feel that his encouragement and support gave me confidence and helped me

My dad used to say, "Women have so much power, and it is a shame they don't use it."

28

develop an invaluable sense of myself. It is unusual for a father to support and encourage a daughter to think and speak freely in this particular culture. At times my mom used to try to warn my dad about all this free thinking business by saying, "We would not be able to marry her off if she starts thinking too much about everything." I feel fortunate to have parents who were looking out for me in their own wise ways. I have been careful raising my children because I know what an influence a parent can be. As parents, we have all the power to influence our children's lives and provide direction. I have always been very keen on making the most of it. Parenting has been an incredible experience and I love it. Not that challenging moments are scarce by any means, but it is all worth it in the end.

Growing up under the influence of strong women was a blessing. I don't think that any school could have taught me the things that I learned from the women in my family. I have the deepest regard for them. I admire their sense of self, strength, wise words and the way they took charge of situations. It was really amazing to see the bond between them and their support for each other.

There is an old bonding tradition where close female friends exchange their scarves. The ceremony is quite enjoyable. All the women get together and then the two women who would like to be the Scarf Sisters bring a beautiful scarf for each other. After the scarf exchange is made, the new sisters are showered with blessings and then everyone has tea, delicious samosas and other appetizers. I am very fortunate to have my own group of Scarf Sisters, here in Madison. These women are a lot of

There is an old bonding tradition where close female friends exchange their scarves.

fun. We stay in touch and make time to go out to dinner at least once a month. Those nights are one of my favorite nights. We sit around for hours, give each other a hard time and have tons of fun. I just love it!

Education for Women

It was common for women of my generation to pursue higher education in our family. However, the purpose was not to acquire education to start a career but rather to stay busy until a 'good marriage proposal' comes along. Families would shy away from educating their daughters to higher levels because then they would not be able to find suitable matches for them. The husbands are supposed to be more educated than the wife, in theory to keep the balance of power in the family. I am grateful to my parents for providing me with the opportunity to go to a private school, even though it was much more expensive compared to the public schools. In fact, my first school was an English convent. That is where I learned English, which has been an asset since I have been living in the west for more than twenty years. I don't know what I would have done without the language skills. I believe language is the biggest cultural barrier for many people who come to a foreign country and culture.

Servants

I was fortunate to live in a home where we had servants to take care of everyday household duties, and a full time cook. The cook would make three different meals everyday. All I had to do was help Mom to come up with a menu for the day and the rest was taken care of, it was quite fun! I do miss that. Sometimes, when I had a long day at work, I really wish someone could make me a hot cup of tea. My life would be complete and I will be ever so grateful, but no such luck here. Our cleaning lady would come everyday,

clean and mop the whole house and clean all the bathrooms. All the bedrooms had an attached dressing room and a bathroom. It took me a while to adjust to the concept of having one or two bathrooms for the whole family.

Mom was always very kind and generous to all the servants and we were expected to do the same. She would get a couple of outfits made for the servants every season. On special occasions, she would go to the market and buy different color flip-flops for them to wear during summer. It is interesting to see people wearing flip-flops around town in summer here, they were mostly used by the servants or in homes as spare slippers only to go to the bathroom and were left by the bathroom doors. I cannot imagine wearing them outside the home. My mother would have a fit if I wore a pair of flip-flops in public, strange world!

The cleaning lady had four kids and during the ten years that she worked at our house had four more. Mom would often talk to her about taking care of herself. She would give her extra money to buy milk and fruit for herself. Two of the servants lived in the back of our house in the *servant's quarters*. There were two separate units each with kitchen and bathroom, they shared the backyard and grew their own vegetables. However, the men ate at our house as they worked there and sometimes on special occasions took food home with them for the family. The cook lived alone because his family lived about two hundred miles away in a village. The other servant was the cook's assistant. He chopped the vegetables and did grocery shopping and lived with his wife and two young kids.

Our oldest servant, who all of us kids referred to as *Mama*, was with our family since he was seven years old. Grandmother adopted him and brought him to

Pakistan when migrating from India, with the rest of the family. He took care of all of us and was always treated with great respect. He married this lovely woman called *Noor Janath*, which means *light of heaven*. She lived and worked at my grandmother's house with her husband. They had two daughters and a son. *Mama* also had a son from his first marriage, I think his first wife passed away only a few years after they got married. Mom trusted *Mama* to come and teach me to cook some of the authentic dishes. Time to time he would come and make me watch him cook some of the food. *Mama* passed away almost twelve years ago. All his kids are married and have their own families. His widow is still being taken care of by our family and her children. The gardener used to come twice a week and take care of the garden. Dad liked to garden, he'd plant vegetables and flowers in his spare time. His special flowers included, black and violet roses. They were always treated with great care. Since I moved away from home, I had to learn to mow the lawn and do other house chores. It has been quite an experience!

Sometimes other family members of the servants would come and ask Mom for financial help. I remember one incident quite clearly. A cousin of the cleaning lady was desperate. Her daughter was getting married and the daughter's new mother-in-law was not very happy with the sari given to her as a gift by the bride's family. The poor woman was in tears and worried that if the mother-in-law would not be happy then she would make things harder for her daughter once the wedding was over. Mom took out one of her beautiful navy blue saris with some silver work on it and gave it to her. The woman was over the moon! The next time the cleaning lady was in, I remember she was very excitedly telling my mom about how the new mother-in-law was so happy with her gift and gave the bride a big hug. All the other relatives were impressed with the bride's mother's thoughtfulness and choice of gifts.

Street Sellers

Choori Wali

Chooris are the colorful beautiful glass bangles and *Choori wali* means a woman with bangles. In Pakistan you can buy them in shops and it is also quite common for women to bring them in huge baskets to sell from door to door. They walk around street from street calling, *"lay Lo Choorian, kaanch Ki Choorian."* What that means is, *'take bangles, glass bangles.'* Women in the household try different bangles and haggle with the seller for better prices. Depending on the number of sets bought, a good price can be negotiated. The woman who used to come to our house became a part of the family. She was fascinated by the refrigerator. Not many families had the luxury of owning a refrigerator, most people used clay vessels to keep the water cold. Sometimes I felt that was one of reasons she actually stopped by at our house, to have a cold glass of water from the refrigerator. Mom always made sure she got plenty of iced water in summer and a hot cup of tea in winter.

I like to wear a lot of bangles, usually somewhere from 12 to 24 at a time. They are sold in sets of twelve, eighteen or twenty-four. The challenge in Pakistan is to see as to who can put on the smallest size bangles. Smaller size bangles are a symbol of soft and delicate hands, which is considered a sign of feminine beauty in Pakistan. Bangles are an integral part of all the festive occasions and day-to-day dressing up for women. They come in vivid colors and are decorated with tiny mirrors and intricate patterns. Married

Smaller size bangles are a symbol of soft and delicate hands, which is considered a sign of feminine beauty in Pakistan.

women must wear bangles all the time because it is seen as a sign of honoring their marriages. I remember the older women would immediately notice and I will be reprimanded if I was not wearing any bangles, once I was married.

In contrast, there is a tradition of breaking the bangles when a woman becomes a widow. It promotes and affirms the message and common belief that a woman's life is over without a man. Divorced or separated women are treated the same way. There is an unspoken strict code of behavior and expectations. Stepping out of the defined roles and guidelines can be detrimental to women's lives. They are seen as the honor of the family and placed on a pedestal. Men of the family have the responsibility to make sure women are well protected.

Kayla Wala

Kayla means bananas and *wala* means man. Once a week usually during the day, a man selling bananas would roam around the streets carrying a basket full of fresh, ripe bananas on his head. He knew who his usual customers were and would stop by at those homes regularly. In Pakistan bananas are almost half the size of what I see here; however, I still remember how fragrant they used to be. Bananas, oranges, lemons and limes are sold in dozens. It was interesting to see that here in America, everything is sold by weight, even bananas and oranges. If you ever get a chance to visit Pakistan, just remember not to ask for a few pounds of these fruits, you might get some weird looks.

Bhutta Wala

Bhutta means corn. Almost everyday a man selling whole corns would walk around the streets. My brother Sohail and I used to wait every afternoon and run out of the door as soon as we would hear him. My brother Nadeem never wanted to come with us, he was too sophisticated for this kind of food. The man used to walk around with a little cart filled with hot sand and all the corns buried in it, which is how they were cooked. The corn man would pull out a corn, peel off the jacket and rub it with a mixture of fresh lemon juice, salt and chili powder, yummy! Sohail and I would sit in the back porch and eat our hearts out. My mouth is watering as I am writing this. I do really miss that.

Unday Wala

Unday means eggs. Sometimes a man would come to the house to sell eggs. He was always very confident that his eggs were farm fresh and we can certainly do the 'ultimate test'. The ultimate test was to put the eggs in a bowl of water, one by one. If one floats to the top then that was a bad egg and he would not charge anything for that one. However, most of the eggs did not float and that would certainly keep him smiling. He would look at us with great pride and say, *"Told you so, my eggs are very good and healthy"*. He was quite a character.

There were other street sellers, like the man who used to bring beautiful fabrics of many different kinds and someone who used to come once a quarter to sell dishes and glasses. When I think about all these people coming to our home to sell their goods, they were actually running a small business, with whatever resources they had available to them. They were making a living, supporting their families and carrying on with their lives. There were many economic and political problems in the country during those years. What I learned to appreciate was that everyone carried on with their lives regardless of all the poverty, wars and political instability in the region. Regardless of the problems they had to deal with, people cared about other people in their lives, were always hospitable and generous. It was not unusual for someone to offer whatever he or she had, to help others out.

MEAT DISHES

Chicken Tikka
Recipe on page 58

Dal Ghosht
BEEF COOKED WITH SPLIT PEAS

1 cup split peas or chana dal
1 pound boneless beef, cubed
1 large onion, chopped
3 large tomatoes, chopped
2 teaspoons garlic, minced
1 teaspoon ginger, minced
2 cloves
1 large cardamom
2 small cardamoms

2 inch cinnamon stick
½ teaspoon garam masala
½ teaspoon chili powder
1 teaspoon ground coriander
½ teaspoon salt
½ cup fresh cilantro, chopped
3 cups warm water
3 tablespoons cooking oil

Heat the oil in a saucepan, add all the whole spices. Add onions; when they turn light brown, add garlic and ginger. Stir the mixture for just a couple of minutes and then add the beef. Stir the mixture for a few minutes. The beef will leave some water. Add all the powdered spices and chopped tomatoes. Let the mixture cook on medium heat for about 10 minutes then add the split peas and 3 cups of water and chopped cilantro. Once the mixture comes to boil, lower the heat and cover the saucepan. Leave it to cook for about 45 minutes or until the beef is tender. Garnish with fresh chopped cilantro and serve with pulao rice.

A very popular dish especially during winter months.
You can substitute lamb for beef.

Palak Ghosht
Beef Cooked with Spinach

1 pound beef, cubed
1 pound fresh chopped spinach
2 medium tomatoes, chopped
1 medium onion, chopped
1 teaspoon garlic, minced
½ teaspoon ginger, minced
2 cloves
2 small cardamoms
1 large cardamom

2 inch cinnamon stick
1 teaspoon chili powder
1 teaspoon garam masala
1 teaspoon ground coriander
¼ teaspoon turmeric
½ teaspoon salt
3 cups of lukewarm water
2 tablespoons cooking oil

Heat oil in a saucepan, add whole spices and then the chopped onion. Stir until it turns light brown. Add ginger and garlic. Add a little bit of water if the mixture starts to stick. Add all the powdered spices and continue to stir. Add chopped tomatoes and keep stirring until the mixture turns brown. Add beef and let it cook for a few minutes. Add water, cover and simmer on medium heat for about 45 minutes, until the beef is almost tender but not quite. Stir in the spinach. Cover and let it cook for another 15 minutes, until the spinach is cooked and all of the water is gone. Serve with pulao rice and dal.

Aloo Ghosht
Spicy Beef with Potatoes

1 pound beef, cubed
2 medium potatoes, peeled and cubed
2 medium tomatoes, chopped
1 medium onion, chopped
1 teaspoon garlic, minced
½ teaspoon ginger, minced
2 cloves
2 small cardamoms
1 large cardamom

2 inch cinnamon stick
1 teaspoon chili powder
1 teaspoon garam masala
1 teaspoon ground coriander
¼ teaspoon turmeric
½ teaspoon salt
¼ cup cilantro, chopped
3 cups of lukewarm water
2 tablespoons cooking oil

Heat oil in a saucepan and add chopped onions, cloves, small cardamoms, large cardamom and cinnamon stick. Stir until it turns light brown. Add ginger and garlic, add a little bit of water if the mixture starts to stick. Add all the powdered spices and continue to stir. Add chopped tomatoes and keep stirring until the mixture turns brown. Add beef and let it cook for a few minutes. Add water, cover and simmer on medium heat for about 45 minutes, until the beef is almost tender but not quite. Stir in the potatoes and cilantro. Cover and let it cook for another 15 minutes, until the potatoes are cooked and most of the water is gone.

Serve with pulao rice and raita.
You can substitute lamb for beef.

Aloo Keema
Ground Beef with Potatoes

1 pound lean ground beef
2 medium potatoes, peeled and
    cubed
1 medium onion, finely sliced
2 medium tomatoes, chopped
1 teaspoon garlic, minced
½ teaspoon ginger, minced
4 dried red chilies

½ teaspoon salt
2 cloves
2 small cardamom
1 large cardamom
2 inch cinnamon stick
¼ cup cilantro, chopped
2 tablespoons cooking oil
1 cup warm water

Heat oil, add all whole spices, red chilies and onions. When red chilies turn deeper in color, add the ground beef. Stir everything together and then add garlic, ginger and salt. Let the mixture cook for a few minutes and then add the tomatoes and potatoes. Allow the mixture to cook in the water left from tomatoes and ground beef, for about ten minutes. Add a cup of water, cover and let it simmer for 10 minutes until the potatoes are cooked. Garnish with fresh chopped cilantro and serve with matar pulao or pooris.

Shami Kebab
GROUND BEEF PATTIES

2 pounds ground beef
½ cup dried yellow split peas
1 onion chopped
1 tablespoon fresh garlic,
    chopped
½ tablespoon fresh ginger,
    chopped
2 large cardamoms
3 small cardamoms

4 inch cinnamon stick,
    broken in half
2 cloves
6 dried red chilies
¾ teaspoon salt
2 cups water
1 egg
½ cup cilantro, chopped
2 cups cooking oil for frying

Add ground beef, onions, ginger, garlic, all spices, split peas and water. Leave it to cook for about thirty minutes on medium heat. Switch off the heat once all the water is evaporated and the meat is brown. Once the mixture cools down, grind it in the food processor to a finer texture. Add egg and cilantro. Mix everything together, then take a ball of ground beef and press it to make a patti about 2 inches wide and ½ inch thick. When all the mixture is made into patties, warm the oil in a deep frying pan. Once the oil is hot but not smoking then add the patties. Be careful about not putting too many in at the same time. Depending on the size of the frying pan, 4-6 patties would be perfect at a time. Turn them over when brown on one side and take them out when both sides are nice and brown. This makes about 12 patties.

My son Samir loves the shami kebabs with pooris.
They are also very tasty when served with
Basmati rice and a delicious yogurt sauce, raita.

Kofta
BEEF MEATBALLS

1 pound lean ground beef
1 medium onion, chopped
3 medium tomatoes, chopped
½ teaspoon garlic, minced
½ teaspoon ginger, minced
2 cloves
2 inch cinnamon stick
1 large cardamom
2 small cardamoms

1 teaspoon garam masala
1 teaspoon chili powder
½ teaspoon salt
½ teaspoon turmeric
½ teaspoon ground coriander
fresh cilantro to garnish
2 tablespoons cooking oil
2 cups warm water

Heat oil in a saucepan, add whole spices and then chopped onions. When onions are sautéed and light brown, add garlic and ginger. Let it cook for a couple of minutes and then add half of all the ground spices. Keep stirring and then add chopped tomatoes and after stirring for a couple of minutes add 2 cups of warm water and leave it to cook on medium heat.

In a separate bowl, mix ground beef and the rest of the ground spices. After mixing it well, make the meatballs and start dropping them in the simmering mixture. Let all the balls cook for about 15-20 minutes. There should be a little bit of water/gravy left around the meatballs. You can reduce the water by turning the heat high, depending on how much of a gravy you would like. Garnish with chopped cilantro. If you are a cilantro fan, you can add some fresh cilantro to the ground beef before making the balls. Serve with parathas or pulao rice.

Kofta
Photo by Michael Anthony Messner

Haleem

BEEF COOKED WITH A VARIETY OF LENTILS AND SPICES

1 cup masoor dal (red/orange) lentils
1 cup chana dal (split peas)
1 cup moong dal (yellow lentils)
½ cup Basmati rice
1 cup oats
2 pounds stew beef
2 large onions chopped
3 teaspoons garlic, minced
1½ teaspoons ginger, minced
5 large tomatoes
2 cloves
2 large cardamoms
2 small cardamoms
4 inch cinnamon stick
1 bay leaf
1 teaspoon chili powder
1½ teaspoons garam masala
¾ teaspoon turmeric
3 teaspoons ground coriander
2 teaspoons salt
1 cup fresh cilantro, chopped
5 tablespoons cooking oil
8 cups warm water

Heat 3 tablespoons of oil in a saucepan and add onions and whole spices. Fry the onions until they turn light brown. Add garlic, ginger and beef. Stir the mixture for a few minutes and add tomatoes. Continue to stir the mixture until the mixture turns dark brown. Add 5 cups of water, cover the saucepan and let it cook on medium heat until the beef is tender and most of the water is gone.

Wash all the dals/lentils and rice thoroughly. Add 3 cups of water and oats. Let it cook on medium heat, until all the lentils are soft, about 45 minutes. Add the beef mixture to the lentils and mix. Add a cup of water if the mixture is too dry and leave it to simmer for another 15 minutes.

Optional. Before serving the haleem, heat 2 tablespoons of oil in a frying pan, add thinly sliced onions and whole cumin. When the onions turn dark brown, add the mixture to the haleem. Garnish with fresh chopped cilantro. This is usually served with shami kebab and plain yogurt.

Bihari Kebab
BEEF FILET ON SKEWERS

3 pounds of thinly sliced
   beef filet
4 large cardamoms
4 small cardamoms
6 black peppercorns
4 inch cinnamon stick
4 cloves
2 teaspoons whole cumin
6 red dried chilies

1 ½ teaspoon salt
2 medium onions, minced
1 small onion, thinly sliced
2 teaspoons garlic, minced
1 teaspoon ginger, minced
1 medium papaya, peeled and
   minced
½ cup chopped cilantro

Roast all whole spices in an oven, on a baking sheet for 5 minutes at 400 degrees. Allow the spices to cool then grind them in a grinder. Mix all the ingredients, except sliced onions and cilantro, thoroughly with beef. Cover with cling film and refrigerate overnight or at least 12 hours. The papaya is used as a tenderizer. Thread the beef on metal skewers and then place on a medium hot grill. Usually when this is cooked in Pakistan, real coal is used so it smells like charcoal. The meat is taken off from the skewers and then garnished with thinly sliced onions and fresh chopped cilantro before served with parathas or pooris. except the thinly sliced onions and cilantro,

This is a very traditional dish prepared at special occasions
like Eid-ul Azha or at weddings.

Lamb Korma

TENDER LAMB COOKED IN SPICY SAUCE

2 pounds of lamb-cubed meat from leg of lamb including bones
2 medium onions, thinly sliced
2 medium tomatoes, chopped
1 teaspoon garlic, minced
½ teaspoon ginger, minced
1 cup plain yogurt
2 cloves
2 large cardamoms
2 small cardamoms

2 inch cinnamon stick
1 bay leaf
½ teaspoon chili powder
1 teaspoon garam masala
½ teaspoon turmeric
1 teaspoon ground coriander
1 teaspoon salt
3 tablespoons cooking oil
3 cups warm water
½ cup fresh cilantro, chopped

Heat a tablespoon of cooking oil in a saucepan and add sliced onions. Fry the onions until they turn reddish brown. Spread the onions on a paper towel and allow them to cool. Add the brown onions, garlic and ginger in a blender and blend it for a few minutes to a smooth paste.

Add 2 tablespoons of oil to the saucepan and add all whole spices. Add the onion paste and fry everything for a few minutes. Add lamb and continue to fry the mixture for about five minutes. Now add all the ground spices and a spoon of yogurt. Slowly add all the yogurt to the mixture, one tablespoon at a time and keep stirring it. The mixture will turn dark brown. Add chopped tomatoes, cilantro and water. Bring the mixture to a boil and then leave it to simmer for about 50 minutes or until the lamb is tender. Serve warm with pulao rice or parathas.

Do-Piazza
Lamb Cooked with Onions and Whole Spices

2 pounds leg of lamb, cubed
4 medium onions, sliced
5 cloves of garlic, chopped
2 inches fresh ginger, chopped
2 medium tomatoes, chopped
5 dried red chilies
½ teaspoon salt

2 large cardamoms
2 small cardamoms
2 cloves
3 cups warm water
3 tablespoons cooking oil
½ cup fresh cilantro, chopped

Heat oil in a saucepan, add all whole spices, garlic, ginger and onions. Stir everything around until onions are sautéd. Add lamb, tomatoes and salt. Add water and bring the mixture to a boil and leave it to simmer on medium heat for about 40 minutes or until lamb is tender and the sauce is reduced. Garnish with fresh cilantro and serve warm with matar pulao or pooris.

Leg of Lamb

WHOLE LEG OF LAMB COOKED IN TRADITIONAL SPICES

5 pounds whole leg of lamb
4 teaspoons garlic, minced
2 teaspoons ginger, minced
1 small onion, minced
8 oz. plain yogurt
3 teaspoons garam masala

1 ½ teaspoon chili powder
1 ½ teaspoon ground cumin
2 teaspoons salt
½ cup olive oil
1 cup chopped cilantro
1 small onion, thinly sliced

Mix, ginger, garlic, onions, cilantro and all ground spices in a bowl. Add yogurt and mix thoroughly. Place the leg of lamb in a roasting dish and pierce the leg with a fork. Spread the spice mixture over the lamb, cover and leave it overnight in refrigerator.

Heat the oven to 350 degrees. Drizzle the olive oil on lamb, cover with foil and leave it in the oven to cook for about 2 hours. Garnish with chopped cilantro, sliced onions and serve with biryani and raita.

Karahi Chicken
Chicken With Spices, Onions, Green Peppers & Tomatoes

1 pound boneless/skinless
chicken cubed
1 green pepper, chopped
1 large onion, sliced
3 medium size tomatoes,
chopped
1 teaspoon garlic, minced
1 teaspoon ginger, minced
2 cloves

1 large cardamom
1 small cardamom
2 inch cinnamon stick
½ teaspoon chili powder
1 teaspoon garam masala
¼ teaspoon turmeric
½ teaspoon salt
½ cup cilantro, chopped
2 tablespoons cooking oil

Heat 1 tablespoon of oil in a deep pan, add cloves, cardamoms and cinnamon stick, let them sizzle. Add chicken, garlic and ginger. Fry for about ten minutes. Empty all the ingredients in a plate/bowl.

Add another tablespoon of oil and add the sliced onions. Fry them until light brown. Add chopped green peppers and tomatoes. Fry the mixture for about 5 minutes, then add chili powder, garam masala, turmeric and salt. Mix all the spices in the onion mixture. Add the chicken to the pan and gently mix everything together with a slotted spoon. Sprinkle cilantro and cover the pan to simmer for about ten minutes. The sauce will thicken and then it is ready to serve with matar pulao.

Clockwise from top: Matar Pulao,
Karahi Chicken, Milli Sabzi & Raita
Photo by Michael Anthony Messner

Chicken Tikka
ROASTED CHICKEN PIECES MARINATED IN YOGURT AND SPICES

6 chicken breasts, skinned
1 cup plain yogurt
1 teaspoon garam masala
½ teaspoon chili powder
½ teaspoon ground cumin

½ teaspoon salt
¼ cup cilantro, chopped
2 tablespoons olive oil
1 small onion, thinly sliced
pinch of red food color

Wash and dry chicken legs and place them in a mixing bowl. Add all spices and food coloring to the yogurt. Rub the mixture on the chicken, cover and leave it overnight in the refrigerator.

Heat the oven to 350 degrees. Place the chicken in a roasting pan, drizzle the olive oil on the chicken and it in the oven for about an hour, or until it is fully cooked. Garnish with cilantro and sliced onions. Serve with pulao rice and raita.

See picture on page 40

Chicken Curry
CHICKEN COOKED WITH SPICES, ONIONS, GINGER AND GARLIC

1 pound boneless/skinless
    chicken cubed
1 large onion, chopped
3 tablespoons of plain yogurt
1 teaspoon garlic, minced
1 teaspoon ginger, minced
2 cloves
1 large cardamom
1 small cardamom

2 inch cinnamon stick
½ teaspoon chili powder
1 teaspoon ground coriander
½ teaspoon garam masala
¼ teaspoon turmeric
½ teaspoon salt
½ cup cilantro, chopped
2 tablespoons cooking oil

Heat 2 tablespoons of oil in a deep pan, add cloves, cardamoms and cinnamon stick, let them sizzle. Add chopped onions, fry them until a little golden brown. Add chicken, garlic and ginger. Fry for about 5 minutes so that the chicken is not pink anymore.

Add chili powder, garam masala, turmeric, coriander and salt. Keep stirring everything, so that the spices are mixed with the onions and chicken mixture. Add a tablespoon of yogurt at a time until all of the yogurt is used and the mixture looks a little yellowish brown. Sprinkle cilantro and cover the pan to simmer for about ten minutes. The sauce will thicken and then it is ready to serve with pulao.

SECTION THREE

Meatless Days

Both of my parents were born in India and moved to Pakistan as adults. Mom had four sisters and two brothers. One of the brothers, his wife and four children, Mom's older sister with her husband and six children and our maternal grandmother lived in Islamabad, where we lived. One of my mom's sisters lived in Karachi, which is a thousand miles away from where I grew up. The third sister lived in Delhi, a city in India and never moved to Pakistan with the rest of the family. The youngest sister was married to a dentist who was in Pakistani military so they moved around the country a lot, due to his postings to different military bases. The youngest brother lived in England so we only saw him once every few years, mostly at weddings and funerals. Some of my parents' cousins and their families lived close by as well. It was very nice to have all these people around me. There was always something fun going on.

My dad was one of eleven children and the only one to move to Pakistan. There were seven girls and four boys in the family and my dad was the only one to pursue higher education, which my grandmother was not very happy about. She always thought that there was something wrong with this son of hers as he always had his head in the books and wanted to work for other people, while the family is rich enough to hire other people to work for them. My father's side of the family owned a lot of land and she didn't think that her son needed to go to school to make a living. Once Dad finished college in India, he got married and then came to the U.S. and acquired a Master's degree from Ohio University. A few years later he went to England and completed his Ph.D. in parasitology, which is the study of parasites. I admire my father for his determination and dedication to achieve his goals regardless of many obstacles. He was alone in England while pursuing a Ph.D. There were many financial challenges and he had four young children and a wife waiting for him in Pakistan.

While my mom was expecting me, my dad had an opportunity to go to England to pursue his Ph.D. He did not get a chance to see me until I was almost three years old. Obviously, he had a lot of catching up to do on his return from England. All of us kids had grown out of having a dad around. Especially my brother Nadeem. He was not at all happy about our dad disciplining him and his brothers. Finally, after getting tired of the new rules, you can imagine my mother's amusement when he asked: *"Who is this new man in the house and when does he plan to go back to his home? I really don't like him."* He was quite disappointed to hear that the 'new man' is actually our father and would live with us for the rest of our lives. He was still not convinced as to why we need a father, we were doing just fine without him. Nadeem was four years old at the time. After dad's return we moved to Peshawar, which is located by the Afghanistan border and then we finally moved to Islamabad, the capitol of Pakistan.

The Wars

Pakistan fought two wars with India in 1965 and 1971. Those were strange times, as far as I can remember. Our house was painted black to prevent it from shining in the moonlight, and trenches were dug out in front of our house. In the middle of the night during air raids we would run out and sit in the trenches to protect ourselves. My brother Sohail and I would at times crawl out of there to watch all the action in the sky. We could very clearly see the

Indian bombers chased by Pakistani planes and anti-aircraft guns going off. We grew up in times of turmoil so we didn't quite experience fear. It all seemed really interesting and just a way of life.

Our family lived near a dam and the airport, which were hot targets for the enemy planes. The living room furniture was moved to another room and we

We grew up in times of turmoil so we didn't quite experience fear.

had mattresses on the floor. All of us slept in the living room so we could stay together during the air raids. I remember that the refrigerator light bulb was removed to keep the light from shining in the night, in case someone opens the refrigerator door and give away any sign of life to the enemy planes. The war lasted for almost six months, Pakistan conquered a lot of land and captured Indian soldiers as prisoners of war. All of that was returned after the cease-fire.

In 1971, East Pakistan fought to become an independent state, what is now known as Bangladesh. A civil war broke out and the natives of East Pakistan, *Bengalis*, started killing all of the non-Bengalis. Hundreds of thousands of non-Bengalis left their homes and made their way to West Pakistan as refugees. Most of them settled in Karachi, the port city of Pakistan. Taking advantage of the internal problems, India attacked that part of Pakistan. More than 100,000 Pakistani troops were sent to East Pakistan to take control of the civil war and fight India. Soon after that, war broke out on the western border as well. It was a very difficult time for Pakistan. The troops were fighting on two fronts with limited resources. Finally, Pakistani troops had to surrender in East Pakistan and Bangladesh became an independent state. Almost 100,000 Pakistani soldiers were taken as prisoners of war by India.

My Uncle who was a dentist in the military was taken as a prisoner. For the first six months we didn't even know if he was alive. Once we knew where he was in an Indian prison, my aunt was allowed to send some things for him like a sweater, some dried food and toiletries like soap and shaving cream. It was a very difficult time for the family. He returned home after spending two and a half years in the prison. Wars not only claim lives but also affect hundreds of families and leave countries economically crippled. For many years after the wars because of the shortage of cattle, we used to have two *meatless days*, which were every Tuesday and Wednesday of the week. All the meat shops were closed

For many years after the wars because of the shortage of cattle, we used to have two 'meatless days'

during those two days. Sometimes extra meat could be purchased in advance to make up for the two days or only vegetarian dishes were cooked. The men in my family always complained about not having meat dishes but my mom would make the most of the opportunity and ask the cook to prepare a variety of delicious vegetable dishes.

VEGETABLE DISHES

Cholay
Spicy Chickpeas

1 pound dried chickpeas	½ teaspoon chili powder
6 cups water	¼ teaspoon ground cumin
4 medium fresh tomatoes, chopped	2 teaspoons chili blend
1 large onion, sliced	2 teaspoons salt
1 teaspoon whole cumin	¼ cup cilantro, finely chopped
	2 tablespoons cooking oil

Soak dried chickpeas in a bowl, overnight. Next morning, drain the water and wash thoroughly under running water. Then add 5 cups of water and leave the chickpeas to cook on medium heat for about three hours or until the chickpeas are tender but not mushy.

Heat oil in a separate saucepan, add cumin seeds. When they start to sizzle, add onions and fry them until they turn golden brown. Add chopped tomatoes and all the spices. Stir the spice mixture for a couple of minutes and then add the chickpeas to it. Mix everything together. Add finely chopped cilantro and leave it to simmer for about ten minutes. Empty the chickpeas in a dish and sprinkle some cilantro on top before serving. You can use sliced tomatoes and onions on the top for decoration.

Cholay, can be served as a snack with tea or part of dinner, as a vegetarian dish. Some people like plain yogurt on the side to balance out the spices.

See photo on page 66.

Saag Aloo
SPINACH WITH POTATOES

2 medium potatoes, peeled and
  cubed
2 pounds fresh spinach, chopped
1 medium onion, chopped
2 medium tomatoes, chopped
1 teaspoon garlic, minced
½ teaspoon ginger, minced

3 dried red chilies, whole
½ teaspoon turmeric
1 teaspoon ground cumin
1 teaspoon salt
2 tablespoons cooking oil
½ cup warm water

Heat the cooking oil in a saucepan and add the dried chilies and onions. When the onions turn golden brown, add the potatoes. Add garlic, ginger and tomatoes. Continue to stir the mixture and add all the ground spices. Add water and let it cook on medium heat for about 10 minutes or until the potatoes are half cooked. Add spinach, cover and simmer for another 15 minutes. Serve with pulao rice or paratha.

Aloo, Gobi aur Matar ki Sabzi

POTATOES, CAULIFLOWER AND PEAS CURRY

1 medium cauliflower,
cut into florets
4 medium potatoes,
peeled and cubed
3 tomatoes, chopped
1 cup peas
1 teaspoon garlic, minced
½ teaspoon ginger, minced
1 teaspoon whole cumin

1 teaspoon chili powder
¼ teaspoon turmeric
1 teaspoon salt
2 teaspoons ground coriander
2 tablespoons fresh cilantro,
chopped
2 tablespoons cooking oil
1 cup water

Heat oil in a pan, fry whole cumin, ginger and garlic for a minute and add potatoes. Add turmeric, coriander, chili powder and salt. Stir for a few minutes.

Add tomatoes and simmer for about 5 minutes. Add cauliflower and cook on high heat for another 5 minutes. Cover and simmer for about 15 minutes until the vegetables are cooked and most of the water is gone. Add green peas and chopped cilantro. Leave to simmer for a couple of minutes on low heat.

Aloo, Gobi aur Matar ki Sabzi, with Raita
Photo by Michael Anthony Messner

Milli Sabzi
MIXED VEGETABLES

2 medium potatoes, cubed
1 green pepper, seeded and
    chopped
1 medium eggplant, chopped
1 zucchini, chopped
4 medium tomatoes, chopped
½ cup fresh cilantro, chopped
1 medium onion, chopped

1 teaspoon whole cumin
½ teaspoon turmeric
1½ teaspoons chili powder
2 teaspoons ground cumin
2 teaspoons ground coriander
1 teaspoon salt
3 tablespoons cooking oil
1 cup warm water

Heat the cooking oil in a saucepan and add whole cumin. Add onions and fry both of them together. Add the eggplant and continue to stir for a few minutes. Add potatoes, zucchini, tomatoes and green pepper. Stir the mixture for another few minutes and then add all the spices. Add water, cover and let the mixture cook on medium heat for 15 minutes. When all the vegetables are tender, add fresh cilantro and serve with matar pulao and any meat entrée.

Aloo Sabzi
SPICY POTATOES

4 large potatoes, peeled and cut
  in chunks
2 medium onions, chopped
3 tomatoes
1 teaspoon garlic, minced
½ teaspoon ginger, minced
3 whole red chilies, dried
1 teaspoon whole cumin

½ teaspoon turmeric
1 teaspoon ground cumin
1 teaspoon ground coriander
1 teaspoon salt
1 cup warm water
½ cup fresh cilantro, chopped
2 tablespoons cooking oil

Heat oil in a pan and add whole cumin, garlic, ginger and onions. Fry the mixture until it is golden brown. Add all the spices and continue to fry. Add tomatoes and cook until the tomatoes are soft. Add potatoes and water, cover and leave to cook on medium heat for about 15 minutes. When potatoes are cooked, add cilantro and serve with pooris or parathas.

Haray Beans ki Sabzi
CURRIED GREEN BEANS

1 pound fresh green beans
2 medium tomatoes
1 teaspoon whole cumin
½ teaspoon chili powder
¼ teaspoon turmeric

¼ teaspoon ground cumin
½ teaspoon salt
2 tablespoons cooking oil
½ cup warm water

Wash and chop off the top and bottom of the beans and cut into inch long pieces. Heat oil in a saucepan and add cumin seeds. Add the beans, tomatoes and all spices. Stir the mixture for 10 minutes. Add water. Cover and cook on medium heat, until beans are tender. Serve with pulao rice and a meat entrée.

Shahi Dal
LENTIL CURRY

2 cups masoor dal
(orange lentils)
1 small onion, chopped
2 medium tomatoes
½ teaspoon garlic, minced
¼ teaspoon ginger, minced

½ teaspoon chili powder
½ teaspoon turmeric
1 teaspoon salt
4 cups warm water
½ cup fresh cilantro, chopped
2 tablespoons cooking oil

Wash lentils thoroughly. Add 4 cups of water, garlic, ginger and all ground spices. Leave uncovered to cook for 30 minutes on medium heat. Heat oil in a frying pan. Add onions and tomatoes and fry the mixture until the onions are medium brown and tomatoes are soft and add to the lentils. Add fresh cilantro and serve with plain rice or as a soup.

Palak Dal
LENTILS WITH SPINACH

1 cup Moong Dal (yellow lentils)
1 pound fresh spinach, chopped
1 small onion, chopped
½ teaspoon chili powder

½ teaspoon turmeric
1 teaspoon salt
1 tablespoon cooking oil
2 cups warm water

Wash the lentils thoroughly, add warm water and bring to a boil. Add all spices and let it cook on medium heat for about 20 minutes. Add chopped spinach and cook for another 15 minutes. Heat oil in a frying pan, add onions and fry until golden brown. Add the fried onions to the lentils and serve warm with rice.

Shahi Dal
Photo by Michael Anthony Messner

Bund Gobi aur Aloo ki Sabzi
CABBAGE AND POTATO CURRY

2 pounds green cabbage,
thinly sliced
3 medium potatoes,
peeled and cubed
3 medium tomatoes, chopped

1 teaspoon whole cumin
1½ teaspoon ground cumin
1 teaspoon chili powder
1 teaspoon salt
2 tablespoons cooking oil

Heat cooking oil in a saucepan and add whole cumin. When cumin starts to sizzle, add chopped cabbage, ground cumin, chili powder and salt. Cover and leave on medium heat for about ten minutes. Add the tomatoes and potatoes. Cover and leave for another ten minutes until the potatoes are soft and cooked. Serve warm with pulao rice or parathas.

Bindi Bhaji
STIR FRIED OKRA

1 pound fresh okra, trimmed at
head & tail, thinly sliced
3 dried red peppers
1 large onion, chopped

½ teaspoon whole cumin
½ teaspoon cumin
½ teaspoon salt
2 tablespoons vegetable oil

Heat oil in a deep wok and add the whole cumin until it starts to sizzle. Add onions and whole red chilies. Add okra and fry for a couple of minutes. Add the spices and continue to stir the mixture until the okra turns a little crisp and brown. Serve with pulao rice or pooris.

Baigan Bhurta
Roasted Eggplant with Traditional Spices

2 medium eggplants
2 tablespoons vegetable oil
2 medium chopped onions
1 teaspoon minced garlic
1 teaspoon minced ginger

1 teaspoon chili powder
1½ teaspoon garam masala
1 teaspoon salt
½ cup cilantro, chopped

Preheat oven to 450 degrees, pierce the eggplants with a fork in a few places. Place the eggplants on a baking sheet for about forty minutes. When ready, the flesh shrinks and sometimes separates by itself. Peel off the skin when it cools down. Chop eggplant into small pieces and leave in a colander to drain.

In a deep saucepan, heat oil and add whole cumin. Add onions and fry until they turn light brown. Add ginger and garlic and continue to stir to prevent sticking. Add all spices, salt and the chopped eggplant. Stir well and cook over medium heat until eggplant is cooked thoroughly. Garnish with fresh cilantro.

SECTION FOUR

Celebrations

Shab-e-Barat

Shab-e-Barat is the fifteenth day of the eighth month of the Islamic calendar. Some people believe that this is the day when Allah (God) analyzes everyone's actions during the past year. Many people believe that it is the night to pray and ask for forgiveness for any mistakes or misdeeds during the previous year. It is a common belief that there is a tree in heaven, the leaves have everyone's names on them and if the leaf falls that night then that person has completed the journey of life. So, it is a night when life-changing decisions are made by Allah. If you really need something in your life then this would be a good time to pray for it; your wish might even be granted. The day is celebrated by cooking a variety of sweets called *halwas*. There is usually a lot of activity in every home. Different types of halwas are prepared, decorated with chopped almonds, pistachios, raisins and silver paper, it is quite a sight! After the whole day is spent on preparing these desserts, they are shared with the family and friends with great pride. The aromas of halwas at different homes are incredible.

Ramadan

Ramadan is the ninth and the holiest month of the Islamic year. The holy book, *Quran*, was given to the Muslims during this month by Allah to follow, through Prophet Muhammad. Muslims are required to fast from sunrise to sunset for the whole month. People with health conditions and pregnant or nursing women are excused from observing the fasts. Because the Islamic calendar is lunar, the dates move by ten days every year, so the fasting is experienced in every season. It is really tough to fast during the summer months because the days are very long and the inability to drink any water/liquids makes it very challenging. Most people spend more time doing religious activities like going to the mosque more often than usual for prayers or participating in charitable causes. The concept of fasting is not only to starve yourself

The concept of fasting is not only to starve yourself but also to think about life and put things in perspective.

but also to think about life and put things in perspective. Sometimes, we get so busy with the worldly life that the concept of mortality gets lost. Ramadan is the month that reminds everyone of an after life and consequences of our actions in this world.

Many traditional foods are cooked for the evening for *Iftar*, which is the feast to end the fast. Many times we will take the food prepared at our house to one of my aunt's houses and share it. Everyone opens the fast together, traditionally with sweet fresh dates and have lots of food and tea afterwards. The women would gather around and talk about shopping plans for *Eid-ul-Fitr*, which is the big celebration at the end of Ramadan. Every night my mom would ask the cook to soak *jalebi* in milk and leave in the refrigerator for Sehri the early morning feast before sunrise. *Jalebi* is a dessert made of flour, deep-fried and soaked in sugar syrup. We would eat it with parathas, which is fried layered bread, fried egg or omelet, perhaps some leftover meat from the night before and tea. Once all the food is prepared and served on the dining table early in the morning, the cook would quietly knock on our bedroom windows to wake us up for the big breakfast and we will brush our teeth and gather in the dining room. After the breakfast, everyone would say the morning prayers and start to get ready for daily business.

Jalebi
Photo by Michael Anthony Messner

School and work schedules change during this month. Everything starts earlier, shopping and restaurants are closed during the day and open at night. It is hard to observe the religious traditions in America or any other foreign country because nothing changes to accommodate these practices, not that I expect them to. I think that I made the choice to live in a different country and culture and would like to be respectful of the systems and laws of my new homeland.

Eid Ka Chand – New Moon Sighting

After the 29th fast, everyone gets anxious to see if the new moon can be sighted, which signifies the end of Ramadan and beginning of the celebration of Eid-ul-Fitr, the next day. After opening the fast, we would all run upstairs to the rooftop to see if we can see the new moon. Once the new moon is sighted, everyone prays to Allah for the gift of a wonderful month of Ramadan and congratulates each other for being a part of their lives. After all the religious stuff is taken care off, planning for the celebrations of Eid begins. Usually, we would have completed all our shopping by then, apart from buying the glass bangles. All the women and girls load up in a car and beg our brothers to drive us to *Moti Bazaar. Moti* means pearls. This bazaar or market is the women's shopping mall. We would always go there to buy bangles, henna and take our outfits to get the embroidery work done. Parking is a huge issue that night because the whole world is there but do we care. Of course not! We make our way through the crowds to the bangle store and start trying on different bangles.

Back at home a traditional menu is prepared for the next day. The traditional dessert is the *sewaee*, which is thin vermicelli cooked in sugar syrup and some in milk with pistachios, almonds and raisins. Other things like samosas, gulab jamun, dahi baras, chaat and many other delicious snacks are prepared for at least 100 guests. Usually, everyone is awake all night for the preparations. It is a very unique experience every year. We used to wait the whole year for that. Kids get all their new outfits including socks and shoes, everything is displayed on a long bench in the corridor of the house, all ready for the next day, dad's things first, then mom and then the kids in the order of their age. I remember the excitement of shopping for new shoes for Eid, about five to ten days before the celebration. I would secretly wear them every night and walk around in my room for a few minutes, wipe them clean and put them back in the shoebox. New outfits and shoes would be bought for all the servants and their families, including the cleaning lady, the man who did the laundry and the gardener.

Once the cooks get busy preparing all the food, the women make tea and paint their hands with henna. Henna takes at least a couple of hours before the hands and feet are stained in a deep red color. However, only married women would paint their feet.

Henna takes at least a couple of hours before the hands and feet are stained in a deep red color.

Sometimes, I would put plastic bags on my hands and go to bed, if I was tired after all the shopping. The color would be a beautiful deep red the next day and lasts for almost seven days.

Eid-ul-Fitr – Day of Celebration

Everyone gets up early in the morning, the men in the family take a shower and get dressed for the special prayers at the mosque. The women usually pray at home so there is no hurry to get dressed. The women of the family start getting ready so that when the men return from the mosque they will be ready to welcome them. My dad will come back and then give us *eiddie*, which is usually money that all the kids get. When my older brother, Sohail, started working we got money from him, too. The most fun was to get money from our grandmother. She would ask one of her grandchildren to go to the bank a day before and get all new, crisp one rupee notes. We all used to gather around her as soon as she would enter the house. She will quietly count the money, press it in our hands, followed by a big hug. She had about twenty-five or so grandchildren at the time. After a big breakfast, people usually start visiting each other's homes and bring gifts for the family, especially for the children.

Eid-ul-Azha

Eid-ul-Azha is celebrated the day after the religious ceremony of Hajj, which is a ten-day pilgrimage. Thousands of Muslims from all over the world gather in the city of Mecca, in Saudi Arabia and perform the pilgrimage. A series of prayers and rituals are performed during the ten-day period and Eid is celebrated on the eleventh day. A lamb or cow is sacrificed in the memory of Prophet Ibrahim and his son Prophet Ismail. Prophet Ibrahim had many consecutive dreams in which he was asked by Allah to sacrifice something precious in the name of Allah. Prophet Ibrahim sacrificed a lamb but the dreams kept recurring in which he was continually asked to sacrifice something dear to him. He realized that this was a test of his faith and after some thought, he gathered the courage and took his son Prophet Ismail to perform the sacrifice, as his son was someone dear to him. He closed his eyes, laid his son down and took a knife to slaughter him. When he opened his eyes, a lamb had replaced his son Ismail and he found his son sitting next to him. He was delighted, he had passed the test.

Usually, a sacrifice of a lamb or cow is made for each adult in the household and sometimes also in the name of people who have passed away. The meat is distributed in a proportion, one-third goes to family and friends, one-third to poor and then only one-third is kept at home and many different dishes are prepared from it. People visit with family and friends, the celebrations continue for three days.

Weddings

Among all the beautiful traditions, weddings are one of my favorite events. Everything is fascinating, the beautiful colors; house full of guests; laughter and delicious food. What is there not to like! No offense to my brothers or cousin brothers but I always enjoyed the weddings of my cousin sisters more. I love my brothers dearly, but it was quite challenging to be the only daughter in the family. I was grateful to have my aunts and cousin sisters to have fun with. It was much more fun because my grandmother, mother, aunts, cousins and myself would spend days shopping and preparing the dowry for the bride, which included somewhere between 51-71 outfits, countless jewelry sets, gifts for the groom's family and outfits for all of us girls for each day of the ceremony. There is not much preparation on the groom's side because the gifts for the bride consists of 15-21 outfits, 2-3 jewelry sets and gifts for the bride's family. For my wedding, my parents asked me to choose 55 outfits. I was ecstatic! The shopping trips started, there was so much work to be done, choosing the fabrics, designing the outfits and the type of work to be done on each outfit, too many decisions had to be made, not that I was complaining at all.

Everything is fascinating, the beautiful colors; house full of guests; laughter and delicious food.

A wedding in Pakistani culture is an elaborate family affair. The wedding customs could be quite different from one region to another. A typical wedding is usually ten days long and each day has its own significance. Different rituals and traditions are observed each day. In the western culture usually all the details of a wedding are organized by the bride and the groom, quite the contrary is true in Pakistani culture where family members take on the role of the wedding planner. Every family member has a role to play and it is his or her pleasure and pride to be a part of the wedding.

The women in the bride's family create the wedding plan, which includes the menu for each day, invitation list, dresses and jewelry for the bride, furniture and household items for the new couple and gifts for the groom and his family to be offered in dowry. The men in the family keep up with the budgetary guidelines, in other words as my dad always used to chuckle and say: *"Our most challenging job is to keep the women from spending everything, as if there is no tomorrow and this is the only wedding they will ever have a chance to organize."*

Most of the marriages are arranged so the bride and groom don't really know each other. The family and its reputation in the community are of the utmost importance. It is assumed that if the family is good, then, the son or daughter of the family would be good as well. That is the reason that families try to stay away from scandals, like extra-marital affairs, divorce, etc. There is a stigma attached to divorce. It is looked upon as a failure of the family rather than just the couple involved and is considered a shame to the family name.

The whole process of matchmaking is quite interesting. As the boys in the family grow up, the sisters take on the role of finding a *suitable* bride for their wonderful brother. They start looking around at weddings and family gatherings. If they find someone attractive enough for their brother, the inquiry starts. The family of the girl is researched and many inquiries are made to find all the relevant information such as, the social

As the boys in the family grow up, the sisters take on the role of finding a suitable bride for their wonderful brother.

class the family belongs to, the family's reputation in the community and the educational background. If everything goes well and all the criteria are met, then it is time for someone to make the connection between the two families. Perhaps a mutual family friend would be the best choice to introduce the two families. The groom's family goes to the bride's house to check them out. They do get an opportunity to see the bride and if they feel this can be a good match, then the marriage proposal is sent. The groom's family usually sends the marriage proposal to the bride's father. The bride's father, after consulting with other elders in the family, and the daughter, accepts or rejects the proposal. If the proposal is accepted then the fun begins. Sometimes, the couple know little or nothing about each other.

Even if the bride and groom had seen each other a few times in the presence of other family members, they never really get a chance to spend time on their own. However, thanks to technology, things are changing. Some families allow the engaged couple to email or talk on the phone. I think that is progress, but dating per se or living together, is still unacceptable. I know that the idea of an arranged marriage is not appreciated in the western culture. The wisdom behind it is two fold. The parents know their children well enough to decide what is best for them and also, the children trust their parent's judgment. In the western culture there is definitely more emphasis on individuality and self-empowerment, all good things, when in balance. I don't think that any system is better than the other but rather, both of them are two extremes. A balance between the two would be ideal. Personally, I feel that there is a bit of romanticism attached to the arranged marriage concept. The early days of marriage are more like the time when people start dating each other, full of excitement and fun. The difference certainly is that in the process of dating, people can decide to go their own way without too much trouble but once you are married then you are pretty much stuck. The couple ties the knot not knowing much about each other. The anticipation of starting a new life with a new partner is quite adventurous. All the work to know each other, discover mutual or not so mutual interests, surprises, pleasant or unpleasant are all part of the process and start once the wedding celebrations are over. Trying to know the new husband is not the only thing that the bride has on her mind. She has to become accustomed with her husband's family members and learn the dynamics of a new family.

Dholki

Three or four days before the wedding, girls and women get together every evening leading up to the wedding. The traditional drum used as the musical instrument is called the *Dhol*. The girls in the family sing traditional wedding songs and practice different dances for the other festive nights of the wedding. *Dholki* is the time for the family to hang out and catch up. The women in the family sit around with sewing jobs, chat, gossip and enjoy tea with delicious snacks. In some families, other family members and close friends host *Dholki* parties at their homes, like a wedding shower.

Mayoun

Mayoun is the very first celebration of the wedding. It is a declaration of the start of the wedding process and is usually five days before the wedding day. The bride and groom are not supposed to see each other from this day on, until

Dancing girls at Mayoun

the wedding day. The bride usually does not leave the house during this week. Her friends and cousins move into her bedroom and keep her company. The bride is dressed in yellow and other women in the family and guests who participate in the ceremony wear different shades of yellow as well. The ceremony starts by relatives putting *Ubtan*, which is a yellow paste on the bride's hands. It exfoliates the skin and leaves it smooth and glowing. It is rubbed on the bride's hands, feet and face everyday until the wedding. The siblings of the parents of the bride bring gifts and sweets for the bride, her parents and siblings.

The bride is brought out of her bedroom under a decorative large red scarf called dupatta, by her brothers, sisters and cousins. Sometimes a swing or a seat decorated with fresh flowers is built for the bride to sit during the ceremony. The elders of the family then approach the bride and feed her some sweets and circle her head with their hands full of money.

Gift giving ceremony for the family at Mayoun

This tradition is called *Sadka*, it is believed to keep the bad spirits away. After the ceremony all the money is put together and given to charity. The cousins and friends of the bride set up the *Dhol*. They start singing wedding songs and dancing. A wonderful feast follows all the singing, dancing and rituals. The quality of the occasion is measured by the quality of food and the menu choices. A similar ceremony happens at the groom's house but the groom does not have to wear yellow, only the women in the family do that.

Ubtan
PASTE MADE FROM NUTS, FLOWERS, OILS AND SPICES

1 tablespoon almond paste
1 tablespoon cashew paste
1½ teaspoon pistachio paste
1 teaspoon heavy cream
1 tablespoon wheat germ oil
1 tablespoon rose water
¼ cup red lentil paste
2 teaspoons gram flour
¼ teaspoon turmeric

Mehndi

Mehndi is the biggest and the most fun partying event of the whole wedding. *Mehndi* is the Urdu word for henna. It creates a temporary tattoo and is used to decorate the hands and feet of the bride. Once mehndi is washed off it leaves a deep red tattoo. The darkness of the tattoo is seen as a sign of the depth of love between the new couple. Usually there are two days of mehndi celebrations. On the first day of the mehndi, beautiful platters or pots of henna decorated with glitter and candles along with sweets and gifts for the bride and her family are brought from the groom's house to the bride's home. The second day of the mehndi, decorated platters or pots of henna, sweets and gifts for the groom and his family are taken from the bride's house to the groom's.

The groom's family and friends bring the mehndi in a procession. Female relatives and friends of the groom hold platters or pots of mehndi decorated with glitter, flowers and candles and walk at the front of the procession. They enter the bride's home singing the traditional songs and are welcomed by the bride's family and friends at the entrance with rose petals and garlands. The women who bring the mehndi

Henna pots at Mehndi

91

dance around the decorated mehndi platters. Competition starts as to which wedding party can perform the best songs and dances. This is the time when all that hard work of practicing at Dholki nights is put to a test. The bride does not take part in the festivities. She is brought out from her room for a little while for the ritual where other happily married women put a bit of

Traditional Mehndi dance.

mehndi on her hand and feed her sweets, so that she will have an everlasting happy sweet married life. After all the singing and dancing, the festivities end in a big feast.

The next day, the bride's family and friends arrive at the groom's house, bringing mehndi and gifts for the groom and his family. Mehndi platters are decorated and the family arrives singing and dancing and is welcomed with rose petals and garlands. The sisters bring the groom under a big decorative scarf and women take turns to put a little henna on his hands while feeding him sweets. The bride's sisters and sister cousins then hold his right hand and ask for money before they let him go. It is a fun tradition. After a bit of haggling and dealing with the groom's brothers and friends the groom pays the sisters and they let go of his hand. The festivities are followed by a delicious dinner organized by the groom's family.

Traditional bride and groom.

The wedding gown for the bride which is traditionally deep red, is prepared by the groom's family although some brides choose pink or gold for their wedding gown. It is a beautiful gown. Usually there is a long skirt, covered with heavy work in gold, a plain silk tunic and either a silk or organza scarf which is also covered in gold embroidery to match the skirt. The second distinctive outfit is for the next day of the wedding and is either gold, turquoise or deep green. This outfit is also covered in heavy gold embroidery. Then there are other outfits, somewhere between 11-19 for the bride. They are a combination of saris and shalwar kameez. Shalwar kameez is a three-piece outfit: the pants are the shalwar, tunic is the kameez and scarf is the dupatta.

The groom's outfit for the wedding consists of an off-white long jacket, white pants and a long white shirt with a gold/silver head gear. A dark suit, a silk tie and white dress shirt is usually chosen for the next day of the wedding.

The Wedding Day

The wedding consists of a reception organized by bride's family. The bride's family invites their own friends and family to the celebration. Usually, the groom's family is asked about the number of guests they would like to bring with them to the wedding. The groups of people who come with the groom are called the *baratis* and are expected to arrive in a procession. Traditionally, the groom's car is decorated with fresh flowers and leads the procession. In olden days the groom would ride a horse and his friends and relatives would be singing and dancing in front of the procession. The bride's family welcomes the procession and greets them with garlands.

The actual religious wedding ceremony is the *nikkah*. The bride and groom stay in separate rooms and both have separate attorneys. The bride's attorney is sent to the bride's room to ask her permission to marry the groom. Once the attorney gets the bride's consent, he returns to the main hall where the groom is seated. The Imam or Holy person who officiates the ceremony confirms the bride's consent by asking both attorneys three times if the bride and groom agree to marry each other. If all the replies are affirmative then a prayer is said to bless the couple for their new lives together. Little packets of dates, nuts and sweet are distributed to all the guests.

Dinner is served after the ceremony and then the bride is brought into the main hall to join the groom. A mirror is placed in bride's lap so the bride and the groom can see each other as a married couple for the first time. The bride's sisters, friends and cousins steal the groom's shoes and

A mirror is placed in bride's lap so the bride and the groom can see each other as a married couple for the first time.

hold it ransom. The groom, his brothers, friends and cousins negotiate a price and the groom has to pay that to the bride's female party. The haggling of the price for the shoes is a lot of fun. Both parties try to negotiate for their own best interest. The money is used by all the sisters and cousins of the bride for going out to eat as a group after the wedding.

Family and friends

Finally, the time comes when the bride has to leave with her new husband and in-laws. It is a sad time for the bride's family and they say their tearful good-byes. The underlying concept is that the bride's family is giving up all rights to their daughter and she will be expected to follow and respect the new rules of her husband's family. The bride is walked to the car while the brother of the bride holds a copy of the holy book *Quran*

Wedding guests

above her head, wishing her a blessed new life. Once the bride arrives at her new home, she is seated next to her husband and showered with gifts by the groom's family. Then the groom's sisters show her to her beautifully decorated bedroom. Usually the groom's friends decorate the bridal suite with fresh flowers, garlands and lights, the day before the wedding.

Valima

Valima is the day after the wedding and is a reception hosted by the groom's family. The bride and groom are brought to the main hall together as husband and wife. There are not many rituals for this day. There is usually a big dinner and the couple is more relaxed and gets a chance to talk to their friends and family. It is quite common for the bride to leave with the members of her family at the end of the ceremony and spend a couple of days at her parent's home. The groom's sisters and cousins arrive accompanied with baskets of sweets and nuts, to bring the bride back to the groom's house after her stay at her parent's house. They are greeted and dinner is served before the bride leaves for her husband's home. The bride is accompanied with more gifts from her family. The gifts usually consist of five outfits and some jewelry for the bride. Traditionally, that is the end of the whole wedding ceremony and most of the guests start leaving for their homes and everyone breathes a sigh of relief after all that hard work.

Weddings in Pakistan are a major affair and I miss attending them. I always tease my children about having a traditional wedding when they decide to get married. They are very kind to support me and say, *"Okay Mom, you can knock yourself out."* It will be my utmost pleasure to be able to organize the weddings and observe the traditions for my children. So, we will see if they still agree with me whenever they decide to get married. Time will tell!

DESSERTS

Rasgullah
Recipe on page 109
Photo by Michael Anthony Messner

Gajar Halwa
CARROT DESSERT

3 pounds shredded carrots
3 pounds granulated sugar
1 can sweetened condensed
   milk
5 green cardamoms
5 cloves

1 cup sliced unsalted almonds
½ cup sliced unsalted pistachios
1 cup dried raisins
1 cup cooking oil
Silver paper sheets *optional*

Leave shredded carrots in a saucepan to cook on low heat in its own water for about two hours. Remove from heat when the carrots turn mushy and darker orange. Heat oil in a separate saucepan and add the cloves and cardamoms. Add the cooked carrots to the oil and start stirring it occasionally. It usually takes about an hour or so and the carrots keep turning darker in color. Add the sugar and a can of condensed milk. The sugar will melt and leave more water in the mixture. Continue to stir the mixture until it turns deep brown and you are able to see the oil on the sides of the saucepan. Add sliced almonds, raisins and sliced pistachios. Keep some almonds and pistachios to decorate. Empty the halwa in a dish and sprinkle the almonds and pistachios on top, and decorate with silver paper. Serve warm with cream.

Chandi Ka Waraq, *silver paper is edible*
and it is used for decoration on special occasions.

Chana Dal Halwa
DRIED SPLIT PEA DESSERT

2 pounds dried split peas
2 pounds granulated sugar
5 cups water
1 can sweetened condensed
   milk

4 cloves
4 green cardamoms
1 cup sliced unsalted almonds
1 cup sliced unsalted pistachios
1 cup cooking oil

Wash the split peas thoroughly and place in a saucepan to cook with water until the mixture is soft and most of the water is gone. Allow the mixture to cool. Place the split peas mixture in the food processor and grind it to a smooth paste.

Add oil to a saucepan, add cloves and green cardamoms, then add the split peas mixture and start stirring. It takes about an hour or so of constant stirring, while the color gets darker then add sugar and a can of condensed milk. Keep stirring for about another half hour. The mixture will be dark brown and will start to leave oil on the sides of the saucepan. That is a sign that the halwa is almost ready. Add almonds and pistachios, keeping some for decoration. Empty the halwa in a dish and sprinkle the rest of the almonds and pistachios on top. Serve warm with cream.

Sooji Halwa
Semolina Dessert

2 cups medium grain semolina
2 cups granulated sugar
2 green cardamoms
2 cloves
½ cup almonds, chopped

½ cup unsalted pistachio
   nuts, chopped
2 cups water
2 tablespoons cooking oil

Heat oil and add cardamoms and cloves on medium heat. A couple of minutes later add semolina and keep stirring it to make sure the semolina does not stick to the pan. Add sugar and water in a separate pan and leave it on medium heat. Once the semolina starts to turn light brown, add the sugar syrup to the semolina mixture and cover immediately. The sugar syrup is absorbed by the semolina mixture very quickly. Remove the saucepan from heat and stir the almonds and pistachios into the semolina mixture. Save a little of both nuts to garnish. Empty the dessert in a bowl and garnish with almonds and pistachios and serve hot or cold with cream.

This is my daughter Sabah's favorite dessert.

Shahi Tukra
Pakistani Bread Pudding

6 slices of white bread,
   cut in half
1 can sweetened condensed
   milk
2 green cardamoms
2 cloves
½ cup chopped almonds

½ cup chopped unsalted
   pistachio nuts
2 cups sugar
2 cups water
Few drops of red food coloring
1 cup cooking oil
1 cup whipped cream

Heat 2 tablespoons of oil in a frying pan and fry the bread slices, two at a time. Keep adding a little bit of oil every time because the bread will absorb all the oil very quickly. Heat sugar, water, cardamoms and cloves in a separate saucepan on medium heat to make sugar syrup. After about fifteen minutes, add condensed milk and food coloring to the sugar syrup. Leave the sugar syrup on medium heat for another fifteen minutes to thicken, but just make sure that the syrup doesn't get too thick because then the bread will not absorb it. Add fried bread pieces to the sugar syrup and remove the saucepan from heat and let it sit for a few minutes. Once all the liquid is absorbed by the bread, gently remove the bread pieces from the saucepan and place in a dish. Garnish with chopped almonds and pistachios. Serve warm or cold with whipped cream.

Sewaee

VERMICELLI COOKED IN SUGAR SYRUP

1 pound vermicelli	½ cup walnuts, chopped
2 cloves	1 cup raisins
2 small cardamoms	2 cups of sugar
1 cup almonds, sliced	2 cups water
1 cup unsalted pistachios, sliced	4 tablespoon cooking oil

Heat oil in a saucepan and add the cloves and cardamoms. Break the vermicelli in small pieces and add to the saucepan. Stir the vermicelli around on medium heat until they turn caramel brown. Add sugar and water in a separate saucepan and leave on medium heat to make the sugar syrup. When all the sugar is dissolved, add the sugar syrup to the vermicelli. Cover the saucepan and let everything cook for about 5 minutes, until all the syrup is absorbed. Remove from heat and stir in all the nuts and raisins. Save some almonds and pistachios to garnish. Serve warm or cold with whipped cream.

This dessert is traditionally served
at Eid-ul-Fitr and Eid-ul-Azha.

Gulab Jamun

DRIED MILK BALLS IN SUGAR SYRUP

2½ cups dried milk powder
½ cup all-purpose flour
¼ cup semolina
3 cups sugar
2 small cardamoms

1 egg
4 cups water
¼ teaspoon baking powder
2 tablespoons sliced almonds
2 cups cooking oil

Bring the water, sugar and cardamoms to boil. Remove from heat when all the sugar is dissolved and set aside. Mix the milk powder, flour, semolina, baking powder and egg and knead the mixture until it forms a soft dough. Take a teaspoon of the dough and make a small ball. Make balls with the remaining dough. Heat oil in a frying pan and fry the balls until golden brown.

Remove with a slotted spoon and transfer the balls into the warm sugar syrup. Make sure that the sugar syrup is warm when adding the fried balls so they absorb the syrup properly. Sprinkle sliced almonds on top and serve chilled or warm with whipped cream.

Rasmalai
Ricotta Cheese Balls in Sweet Milk

2 pounds ricotta cheese
½ cup sugar
5 cups half & half
¼ teaspoon crushed
    cardamom seeds

½ cup blanched almonds
2 tablespoons chopped
    green pistachios

Crush two green cardamoms and set the seeds aside. Mix cheese, sugar, and half of the crushed cardamom seeds. Spray a baking tray with baking spray and spread the mixture about an inch thick on a baking tray. Heat oven at 350 degrees and bake for 35 minutes or until it sets. The mixture should not turn brown. Remove from oven, cool at room temperature and cut into 2 inch squares. Place them in a dessert bowl. Heat but not boil half and half, almonds and the rest of the cardamom seeds in a separate saucepan and pour over the squares. Garnish with pistachios. Chill for 2-3 hours and serve.

Rasgullah
CHEESE BALLS IN SUGAR SYRUP

4 cups whole milk
1 teaspoon white flour
2 cups sugar

2 cups water
6 teaspoons fresh lemon juice

Heat the milk to boiling point and add lemon juice for curdling. When milk is completely curdled, pour into a muslin cloth and allow to drain. Press the cloth with a weight and leave to drain completely. Once the solid cheese has been formed, add flour and knead to a soft dough. Make small balls from the dough. In a pan, boil sugar and water for 5 minutes to make a syrup and carefully drop the balls into the syrup. Cook the balls gently in the syrup for 15 minutes. Garnish with almonds and pistachios. Serve chilled with the syrup.

See photo on page 98.

Kheer
RICE PUDDING

1 cup long grain rice
1 can sweetened
    condensed milk
3 cups whole milk

½ cup sugar
Chopped almonds and pistachios
2 cups water

Wash rice and cook in water for 10-15 minutes on medium heat. Add condensed milk, sugar and whole milk. Cook for another 15 minutes, stirring continuously, until the kheer thickens in consistency. Remove from heat. Pour into a bowl and garnish with chopped almonds and pistachios. Serve cold or warm.

SECTION FIVE

Jasmine in Her Hair

Most of my life, I saw Mom dealing with many health problems. Over the years she lost her eyesight. It all started in her early thirties. It was really hard to see her go through endless tests, treatments and hospital visits. I loved her very much and learned to take care of her quite early in my childhood. We became close and I always felt this special bond that I still think about and treasure.

There were four children in our family, three boys and myself. My brothers, Pervez, Sohail and Nadeem are all older than I am. I love my brothers, but I always wanted a sister. My brothers used to do things together, so most of the time I felt like the odd one out. Sadly, we lost our oldest brother Pervez when he was only thirteen years old. His death was hard on my parents; after having my own children, I can't imagine if there could be anything worse than losing a child. I was only four years old at the time so have some vague memories about how sad Mom was and when they brought him home from the hospital for the funeral. It was also very hard on my brother Sohail because he was three years younger than Pervez, they used to hang out together. I know that after Pervez passed away, Sohail felt responsible for us two wee ones and took care of Nadeem and me.

Nadeem and I are a year apart in age, so we used to fight a lot. Nadeem was my mom's and grandmother's favorite. They would fuss over him all the time, not that I am jealous or anything. It was all about him. Sometimes my mom would worry that he is so fragile and gets sick really easy. Part of that was true, Nadeem did used to have really high fevers at times. If I was ever sick, I was instructed to take the medication, rest and will be fine soon. God forbid, if Nadeem got sick, the whole household comes to a stand still. The cook is ordered to prepare Nadeem's favorite dishes everyday and he would be in heaven. He loved it when Mom and Grandma would fuss over him like that. It used to be quite a scene, he had them both wrapped around his little finger.

It was apparent to everyone that my parents were very close to each other. They had a set schedule: my dad would come back from work, take a nap in the afternoon, and then they would have tea together around 5 o'clock in the afternoon and discuss their day. Tea was always served with snacks like samosas, pakoras and sweets. Mom would be spending all morning shopping or having tea with my aunts or grandmother but it was very important for her to be back home before my dad comes home from work. She would always make sure that she looks good and throw on a beautiful fresh sari before his arrival. We used to be quite amused by all this, my aunts and myself would tease her at times but she really didn't care about our opinions in this matter and ignored us most of the time.

Tea was always served with snacks like samosas, pakoras and sweets.

Dad used to go on foreign tours at least twice a year. He would bring beautiful gifts for my mom—three saris and a perfume. The evening after dad's arrival back home, mom would try all the new saris, one after the other to show dad. It was fun! Dad had impeccable taste and enjoyed shopping for the women in his life, which were Mom and I. My friends were envious of that and I never hesitated being a show off.

We had a string of jasmine bushes around the house and in the backyard. During spring and summer months the jasmine plants would be covered with beautiful fragrant flowers. I can still remember the fragrance of the jasmine flowers clearly even after so many years. Both of my parents were used to getting up early in the morning. They sat outside and ate breakfast. Dad will be reading his newspaper and Mom would sit there and talk to him about household stuff. Sometimes,

> *I can still remember the fragrance of the jasmine flowers clearly even after so many years.*

if I managed to wake up early and had some time before leaving for school, I would join them. I liked doing that because it was a very pleasant time of day, cool and fresh. I would pick some jasmine flowers and make a garland for Mom to wear in her hair. She had thick long black hair that she used to wear in a braid or a bun. The jasmine flowers looked absolutely beautiful in her hair. Sometimes, if I was in a hurry and didn't have enough time to make the garland, I would just weave them in her hoop earrings. At night, the garland or the flowers from the earrings would go under her pillow, which would leave the bedroom bursting with fragrance. These are some very fond memories.

Although, my mother was not well most of the time she was the hub of our household. My dad would teasingly call her the *Queen Bee* or the *Control Center*, which I think was true. All of us, including dad used to gather around her all the time. She would run the household, manage the servants and make sure that day-to-day household operations ran smoothly. Sometimes I would help her if she was not feeling very well. Being close to my mother taught me a lot of things: perseverance, the quiet strength and the sense of duty towards the family. Most of all, her cheerful and pleasant appearance, regardless of challenges at hand, was outstanding. I am appreciative of that, because these qualities were extremely helpful when I had to fight some of the battles in my life. I was quite surprised when my daughter Sabah said to me a few weeks ago, that growing up she has always seen me very together, even when things at home were not going very well for us as a family or I was upset. I was surprised by her comment and then it dawned on me, that I never realized how well I have learned that from my mother. No matter what was happening in our lives, it was always a priority for her to make sure that day-to-day life goes on and every day was a new day.

It is a shame that my mother passed away almost 21 years ago when she was only 52 years old. Losing her was a big blow for all of us. Mom's death was the hardest on my dad. He was heartbroken and barely lived for another three years. It felt as if suddenly I have been thrown into a desert under a burning sun without any shade around. I felt lost for a long time. Coming to terms with losing loved ones and someone so special is one of the biggest challenges in life.

RICE &
BREAD DISHES

Clockwise from upper right:
Paratha, Matar Keema, and Dahi Baras

Paratha
Fried Layered Bread

3 cups white/wheat flour
2 cups warm water

½ teaspoon salt
1 cup oil for frying

Mix the flour with water and salt. Knead the ingredients into a soft pliable dough. Divide the dough equally into balls. Roll out each ball and apply oil on it, then turn the edges inwards to make a square. Press and roll the square again. Place the paratha on a hot flat pan and drizzle oil on one side. When the side turns brown turn it over and drizzle oil on the other side, until both sides are brown. Serve hot with any vegetable or meat curry.

See picture on page 116

Poori
Deep Fried Bread

3 cups white/wheat flour
1 teaspoon salt

2 cups warm water
3 cups cooking oil

Add water and salt to the flour and knead it into a dough. Cover and leave for about 30 minutes. Then knead it again so the dough is soft but not sticky.

Divide the dough into golf size balls. Roll out the balls in about 4 inch circles. Heat oil in a deep frying pan and fry the pooris, 2 at a time. Serve warm with any vegetable or meat curry.

Aloo Paratha

Fried Bread Stuffed with Spicy Potatoes

2 large potatoes, boiled,
  peeled & mashed
2 cups plain/wheat flour
2 green chilies, chopped *optional*
1 cup green onions, chopped
½ cup cilantro, chopped

2 teaspoons salt
½ teaspoon chili powder
½ teaspoon ground cumin
2 tablespoons cooking oil for
  frying

Add chopped cilantro, green chilies, green onions, ground spices and 1 teaspoon salt to the mashed potatoes. Mix well and keep aside. Mix flour with a teaspoon of salt and knead to make a smooth dough. Divide the dough into small parts. Make a well in each small round of dough and fill it with potato mixture. Close the well and roll out into a circle.

Heat a flat pan and fry the paratha on both sides. Serve hot with any main meat or vegetable dish.

Matar Pulao

Rice with Peas

2 cups uncooked Basmati rice
½ cup frozen peas
2 cloves
1 large cardamom
1 small cardamom

1 bay leaf
2 inch cinnamon stick
½ teaspoon salt
pinch of turmeric
1 tablespoon cooking oil

Wash rice thoroughly and leave to soak for 15 minutes. Heat oil in a pan, add the whole spices. Let them sizzle for a minute. Add green peas and salt. Add rice and 3 cups of water. Let it come to a boil and then reduce heat and leave to simmer for 15-20 minutes. Add a pinch of turmeric for color. Serve with Karahi Chicken.

Pulao

Rice Cooked with Onions and Whole Spices

2 cups uncooked Basmati rice
1 small onion, chopped
1 tablespoon cooking oil
2 cloves
2 inch cinnamon stick

1 large cardamom
1 small cardamom
1 bay leaf
salt

Wash rice thoroughly and leave to soak for 15 minutes. Heat oil in a pan, add the whole spices. Let them sizzle for a minute. Add chopped onions and fry them until light brown. Add rice and 3 cups of water. Let it come to a boil and then reduce heat and leave to simmer for 15-20 minutes. Can add a pinch of turmeric for color. Serve with chicken curry.

Lamb Biryani

FRAGRANT RICE COOKED WITH TENDER LAMB

2 pounds leg of lamb, cubed
1 large onion, sliced
1 large onion, chopped
3 green chilies
1 teaspoon garlic, minced
½ teaspoon ginger, minced
3 tablespoons ground coriander
1 teaspoon chili powder
2 teaspoons garam masala
1 teaspoon salt
1 large cardamom
1 small cardamom

2 cloves
3 peppercorns
2 inch cinnamon stick
2 bay leaves
Few saffron threads, soaked in 2
    tablespoons of milk
2 cups plain yogurt
4 cups Basmati rice
10 cups warm water
½ cup chopped cilantro
4 tablespoons cooking oil

Marinade lamb in 1 cup of yogurt and leave for a couple of hours. Mix chopped onion, garlic, ginger, cilantro and green chilies together in a blender. Heat 2 tablespoons of oil, add all whole spices, except the bay leaves, half the sliced onions and the mixture. Fry everything together for a few minutes and then add meat to the pan and discard the marinade. Fry the mixture for another few minutes and add all the ground spices and remaining yogurt. Add 2 cups of water and cook gently, until the meat is tender. Remove from heat.

In a separate saucepan, heat 2 tablespoons of oil, add bay leaves and remaining sliced onions. Fry the onions until dark brown and then remove them from oil. Add rice and salt to the pan and 6 cups of water. Bring to a boil, cover and let it simmer for about 20-25 minutes, until all the water is absorbed.

Take a large, open deep dish. Add a layer of rice at the bottom, place a layer of lamb and sprinkle with saffron, keep going until all the meat and rice is used. Sprinkle the top with fried onions and cilantro. Serve with raita and shami kebab.

Sabzi Biryani
Vegetable Biryani

2 medium potatoes, peeled
    and cubed
1 cup cauliflower florets
1 large green pepper, chopped
1 cup peas
½ teaspoon garlic, minced
¼ teaspoon ginger, minced
2 bay leaves
3 cloves
2 large cardamoms

2 small cardamoms
2 inch cinnamon stick
½ teaspoon turmeric
1 teaspoon chili powder
½ teaspoon garam masala
1 teaspoon salt
3 cups Basmati rice
2 tablespoons cooking oil
5 ½ cups warm water

Wash the Basmati rice and soak in water for 15 minutes. Heat oil in a saucepan, add all whole spices, garlic and ginger and fry for a few minutes. Add all vegetables and fry for another 5 minutes. Add 1 cup of water and lower the heat for about 10 minutes.

Add all the ground spices and rice. Add the rest of the water, bring to a boil and then cover and simmer for about 25 minutes. Serve warm with chicken or lamb curry.

Tahiri
BASMATI RICE WITH POTATOES

2 medium potatoes, cubed
1 medium onion, chopped
2 medium tomatoes, chopped
1 bunch green onions, chopped
1 teaspoon garlic, minced
½ teaspoon ginger, minced
1 teaspoon whole cumin
1 bay leaf
1 large cardamom
1 small cardamom
2 cloves

2 inch cinnamon stick
½ teaspoon chili powder
½ teaspoon garam masala
¼ teaspoon turmeric
1 teaspoon ground coriander
½ teaspoon ground cumin
1 ½ teaspoon salt
3 cups Basmati rice
2 tablespoons cooking oil
5½ cups warm water
½ cup fresh cilantro, chopped

Heat oil in a saucepan. Add all the whole spices and chopped onions. Fry the onions until golden brown. Add potatoes, tomatoes, green onions, garlic, ginger, cilantro and all the ground spices. Continue to stir the mixture. Add 1 cup of water, cover and let the mixture cook on medium heat for about 10 minutes. Thoroughly wash and rinse the rice and then add to the potato mixture. Add the rest of the water. Bring the mixture to a boil and then cover and simmer for about 20 minutes until all the water is absorbed. Serve with any meat or vegetable dish and raita.

Clockwise from upper left:
Tahiri, Chicken Curry, & Tamater Chutney
Photo by Steve Tesmer

SECTION SIX

New Beginnings

When I look back and think about my life so far, it seems to be quite a journey. I have lived in four different continents. Although there were some difficult times to endure, I still appreciate the fact that I had an opportunity to learn many new things and experience life in many different contexts; not everyone gets a chance to do that.

My family arranged my marriage, which is the norm in Pakistan. I was engaged for almost six months. We saw each other often but always in the presence of other people. After getting married, we left Pakistan and went to Tripoli, Libya because my husband was working at the University. We lived there for four years and then moved to England. My husband was accepted in the Ph.D. program at the London School of Economics. We had our wonderful two-year-old daughter Sabah with us. A year later we were blessed by a son, Samir. I was ecstatic!

Unfortunately, our marriage started to fall apart from then on. It was a scary time because I didn't know who to turn to because my family was far away in Pakistan and I was all alone in a strange country. Traditionally, if a marriage falls apart, the woman is taken in by her family and spends the rest of her life living at the family home. Sometimes, she is married away quickly for economical reasons to husbands who are either much older, divorced or widowed and are looking for a wife and a mother for their children. It is very unfair! I grew up in Pakistan and knew how the system worked, I was determined to learn to support my children and myself after the failure of my marriage. I love my brothers but I would not like them to raise my children and had vowed to do that on my own.

I am a firm believer of the fact that life happens, it doesn't asks you if you are ready or equipped to take the challenge. Decisions made or paths chosen at that time determine the direction in life. Clarity of mind and a vision of the future, which might not be well defined at that point, are the keys to handle adversities in life. Nothing is impossible in my opinion and experience. It entirely depends on the person whether they decide to be the victim of circumstances or step up, take control and prove themselves.

Decisions made or paths chosen at that time determine the direction in life.

Although, I had lost both of my parents but my dad's confidence in me and his encouragement to pursue what feels right, played a major role in making these decisions. I was convinced that it will certainly be a test of endurance but I am capable of handling the situation and making my way through life's challenges with dignity. I was very focused and took the challenge: nothing seemed difficult or impossible. It is truly amazing as to what a determined mind is capable of achieving.

My very first job was at Safeway's Pharmacy in England as a sales assistant. We were living in a small town called Pinner, about twenty minutes away from central London. I had never worked before in my life but was determined to find a job. I was called in for an interview on a Friday afternoon. I was nervous but excited. During the interview I told my boss that I did not have any prior work experience but it will be very kind of her to hire me because I desperately need a job. If things didn't work out, she could fire me within 90 days and I will understand. She offered me the position, starting the following Monday for three pounds an hour, which is about $4.50. I was over the moon!

Within a few months, I was doing inventory tracking, ordering, invoices and reconciliation and got a raise of 75 pence. I worked there for four years and never got fired. About two years or so after working at the pharmacy, it became quite apparent to me that working to support my family would be a long-term issue. It was also obvious that working at the pharmacy would not be enough; I should start looking for something to prepare myself for better opportunities. I saw a flyer offering accounting classes, one day a week at the local university. I knew I was good at numbers so I called and registered for a couple of classes. The cost was 200 pounds and I had three weeks to come up with the payment. It took many extra hours of work but I made it. My boss was happy to give me a day off from work and I started school. At the end of the two years, I could sit for my first ACCA exam, which is similar to the CPA exam here in U.S. but I was only eligible to take the first two papers as a returning adult student. Once I passed those two then I could take the other fourteen. I passed the first two exams with flying colors.

Finally, after many years of marriage I made the decision to leave my husband, my kids and I moved to U.S. It was one of the most difficult decisions of my life. We had to leave our home and all our possessions behind. I came to Wisconsin, with two young kids, no degree or job offer and a few hundred dollars, that was it. Now was the chance of my life to make everything work and start fresh. Our lives had changed completely and lots of challenges lay ahead. It was quite a challenge to move to a new country and experience a new culture. Everything seemed different to all of us.

My brother Nadeem and his wife Catherine were very kind to take us in. I enrolled in a night school right away in a four-year accounting program but had to wait for a year to get a workers permit from the immigration office. Catherine's brother Dennis was kind enough to offer me a bookkeeping job for his new business as soon as I was allowed to work. I am very grateful to him for that.

Almost two years later, my children and I moved out from Nadeem's and Catherine's home to our own apartment. I was delighted to have a home again for the kids and myself. We didn't have much when we moved. It was very nice of Nadeem and Catherine to give us their couch. I bought the beds for all of us and some kitchen utensils, china and silverware to be able to cook and serve a decent meal. Slowly, I started buying other necessities and the apartment started to look more like a home. It reminds me of a bird, how it slowly and patiently gathers each and every stick to make a nest. Every time the storm or strong winds blows it away, it starts all over again but never gives up.

After four years of hard work, I graduated with a bachelor's degree in accounting in December of 1999. It was a special day, this dream had kept me going for all those years. The school was about 40 minutes away from home. Driving home at 9:30 at night after the class was challenging at times, especially during the Spring semester because of the snow and ice on the roads. I had a very old car that a friend had helped me buy for a few hundred dollars. We used to call it the Rex, like the dinosaur. The awful road conditions would make the drive very long and stressful. At times I would get home around 11 o'clock at night. The next morning start at 6 again and get the kids ready for school and go to work.

Now when I look back, it seems impossible but at the time I had the drive, nothing seemed like an obstacle. I was in school full-time, had two jobs at times to make ends meet, I barely had any time to spend with the kids; however, I would get Sundays to spend at home but that was also the day to catch up on housework and cook for the following week. I used to cook 5-6 dishes and freeze them and make rice every morning before leaving for work. It was very important to me that the kids had a home cooked meal when they came back from school. At work, I learned to eat my lunch in ten minutes during the lunch hour and utilize the rest of the break to catch up on homework for school.

It was very important to me that the kids had a home cooked meal when they came back from school.

Acquiring the CPA license was the next step. I started preparing for the exam right after graduation. It took me a little while but I passed the CPA exam and got my license. That was another day of celebration. I feel fortunate to have an opportunity to carve a new life for my children and myself. We have come a long way and the biggest achievement for me is that my children and I are still a family and remain close to each other, we kept it together through the hard and testing times.

People such as I, move to a new country in search of safety and opportunities to start a new life but there is a price for that. Living away from your own family and culture can be very stressful and isolating. It was rough, I feel that it took courage, perseverance and many hardships to get where I am today. I don't have any regrets at all, it was all worth it. I do strongly believe that it would have been much harder if I did not have the support of some very special people in my life like my brothers, their families, my uncle Shamim, his wife aunt Cora and my cousin Tanveer. They mean the world to me. I would always love them for being there for me during challenging times.

Nadeem used to visit us every year in London during the Christmas holidays. In fact, my kids used to call him Santa because he would come during the holidays and bring lots of gifts for them. It was a treat to be able to see him at least once a year. He lives in California now but visits often. It is always wonderful to spend some time together, have dinner or maybe watch a movie and catch up. Thanks to technology, Sohail and I email frequently; it has been great. I have not been home in eighteen years and have yet to meet Sohail and his wife Rizwana's children, Ayesha and Hassan. We email back and forth and I feel fortunate to have an opportunity to be a little part of their lives.

Despite the hardships, moving to the U.S. has been a great experience and an adventure.

Despite the hardships, moving to the U.S. has been a great experience and an adventure, from learning to drive on the wrong side of the road to getting used to calling the 'post', the mail. I had to pay extra attention to the dates and learn to write the dates backwards, month first, then the day and the year. Sometimes the English system would kick in and then none of the accounts for that month would balance at work, as the postings would go to the wrong accounting period. In Europe and Asia the dates are written differently, date first then month and year. It took me a while to get accustomed to the new American way of life. Everything is instant, whether it is hamburger helper or pack of brownies, this is America, just add water!

I enjoy living here because there are many things that I value such as freedom for women, lots of opportunities to follow your dreams and a reasonable cost of living. If you work hard and follow your dreams, anything is possible. I do believe that if you can't live the life of your dreams in this country, then there is no other place on this planet where it can happen. You most likely will have to move to a different planet!

Nadeem and Catherine were the only people I knew, when I first moved here but I have made numerous friends since then. I love to throw big parties and usually the guest list runs from 45-75 people at a time. I feel fortunate to have found delightful friendships that I appreciate and enjoy. Aside from all the very important reasons that I love America, I love shopping; the variety, the never ending weekly sales and most of all end of season sales. I love the wonderful deals, it is more of a game for me to challenge myself to see how cheaply I can buy something. Perhaps there is something weird about this but believe me it is very exciting at the time!

Eight years later, I have a wonderful job as a CPA. I am fulfilling my dream of writing a book and love to teach Pakistani cooking classes. I am starting a new web-based business *White Jasmine* with my dear friend Gail and producing my own television cooking show, *Curry and Coriander*. My children are doing well and they still love me. I have a wonderful family and group of friends, I don't think I can ask for more.

When I look back, my journey of life seems to consist of many challenges and drastic changes in the direction of life. However, as the journey continues, who knows what other challenges are waiting around the corner. One can only keep moving forward with a warm heart and a relentless spirit!

SAUCES & DRINKS

Samosas with various sauces

Raita
YOGURT SAUCE

2 cups plain yogurt
½ teaspoon ground cumin
1 teaspoon whole cumin

¼ teaspoon chili powder
¼ teaspoon salt
¼ cup fresh cilantro, chopped

Beat the yogurt in a bowl and add all the spices. Mix well and add chopped cilantro. Serve cold as dipping sauce with samosas and pakoras or a delicious side sauce with any main entrée. You can add chopped cucumber or green onions to this sauce if you like.

Imli ki Chutney
TAMARIND SAUCE

3 tablespoons dried tamarind
1 teaspoon ground cumin
¼ teaspoon chili powder

1 teaspoon salt
1 teaspoon sugar
1 cup hot water

Put tamarind and hot water in a bowl to soak for about an hour. Squeeze the pulp and take all the seeds out, then strain the liquid. Add salt, sugar and all the other ingredients to the tamarind water and mix well.

Serve as a dipping sauce with samosas and pakoras.
These sauces are also used as a compliment to the entrées.

Dhaniya ki Chutney
CILANTRO SAUCE

1 bunch fresh cilantro	¼ teaspoon salt
2 red dried chilies	1 teaspoon olive oil

Wash cilantro thoroughly, remove the stems and put it in a blender. Add red dried chilies, a teaspoon of olive oil and salt. Blend thoroughly for a couple of minutes. Serve with samosas, pakoras or as a side sauce with main entrée.

Tamater ki Chutney
TOMATO SAUCE

2 pounds of ripe tomatoes, chopped	1 teaspoon whole cumin
1 large onion, chopped	1 teaspoon ground cumin
1 bunch green onions, chopped	½ teaspoon chili powder
1 cup fresh cilantro, chopped	1 teaspoon salt
	2 tablespoons cooking oil

Heat oil in a saucepan and add whole cumin. When cumin starts to sizzle, add chopped onions, all spices and green onions. Fry them for a couple of minutes on medium heat. Add tomatoes and let the mixture cook for about 10-15 minutes. When tomatoes will turn saucy, remove from heat and garnish with chopped cilantro. Serve warm with any main entrée.

Masala Chai
Spice Tea

4 cups water
5 teaspoons dried English
    Breakfast tea leaves
    or 5 tea bags
4 teaspoons evaporated milk

4 teaspoons sugar
1 clove
1 green cardamom
1 inch cinnamon stick

Boil water in a kettle with whole spices. Before pouring the boiled water into the teapot rinse the teapot with hot water.

Add tea leaves or tea bags to the teapot and then pour the spiced boiled water with the whole spices into the teapot. Cover with a tea cozy and leave it to brew for a couple of minutes. Add sugar to the tea cups and then pour the tea. Add evaporated milk, stir and serve.

When using tea leaves, pour the tea concoction through the strainer into the tea cup. Remove strainer and mix the tea well.

Chai

TEA

4 cups water	4 teaspoons evaporated milk
5 teaspoons dried tea leaves or	4 teaspoons sugar
5 teabags of your choice	

Boil water, preferably in a kettle. Before pouring the boiled water into the teapot, rinse the teapot with hot water. Add tea leaves or tea bags to the teapot and then pour boiled water in the teapot. Cover with a tea cozy and leave it to brew for a couple of minutes.

Add sugar to the tea cups and pour the tea into the tea cups. Add evaporated milk, stir and serve.

Mango Lassi

MANGO DRINK

1 cup diced fresh mango	4 tablespoons sugar
2 tablespoons plain yogurt	2 cups whole milk, chilled

Combine diced mango, plain yogurt & sugar in food processor. Blend for 1 ½ minutes. Set aside. Pour milk into processor & process until it becomes frothy. Add the mango puree to the milk and process for about 1 minute. Pour into glasses with some ice cubes.

A very popular drink especially during summer months.

AFTERWORD

It is with gratitude, admiration, and great respect for my mother that I am able to write this afterword for her first book. Since my brother wrote the foreword, I thought it would be appropriate to end the book on the same note.

As a child, I remember the wonderful stories that my mother told me. She would tell me how she grew up, what she saw, and all the instances described in this book. It was only after reading her words, however, that I was able to get a really clear and sound understanding of her experience. A mainstay of life at home always involved her cooking; as I grew up, I became accustomed to the spices, flavors, and uniqueness of traditional dishes. Since I have moved out from home, I have a lot to learn in order to re-cultivate those recipes!

Through this book, I have gained great understanding and insight into the history of my family. Initially, I had no idea that my mother had intentions of writing this by intertwining our family history with it. I can see now how important this was. It has helped me make sense of a culture that I never experienced directly.

I consider the compilation of this book a gift. It is a gift to my brother and me. It is a gift to our family. Yet, it is also a gift to people who may be unfamiliar with the Pakistani culture and traditions. It is both a memoir, but also a very useful cookbook. All of the magnificent recipes are traditional and have been passed down for generations; you will find variations of each dish across different families.

And so, I thank my mother for all she has given me, shown me, and shared with me. It is due to her strength and perseverance that today I can see life with a balanced perspective. She has not only been there for me, but also provided me with unmatchable wisdom and integrity. As the years go by, I see more and more how valuable these gifts are, and I am very grateful. I hope to pass along this book, along with the stories and recipes, to my own family. It can only be through this that we can keep our traditions alive.

Sabah Karimi
Daughter of Huma Siddiqui

About White Jasmine

White Jasmine offers a variety of spices, tea, and fine gifts rooted in the cultural traditions of Pakistan. We believe that in today's international marketplace, providing an opportunity for families and friends to create their own traditions is vital. Our gifts are handmade by highly skilled craftsmen and imported from Pakistan. Our tea and spices are made only from the highest quality ingredients and acquired from some of the best suppliers in the U.S. We insist on high quality, exceptional presentation and outstanding customer service.

Please check out our web site for more information about White Jasmine.

www.whitejasmine.com

About Curry and Coriander

Curry and Coriander with Huma is the first Pakistani cooking show series produced in Madison, Wisconsin. *Curry and Coriander* offers an opportunity for people to learn about traditional spices, authentic dishes, and hear stories of Pakistani culture.

Please check out our web site for more information about Curry and Coriander.

www.curryandcoriander.com

MENUS

Typical Lunches

Lamb Korma	Kofta
Plain Rice	Tahiri
Baigan Bhurta	Tamater ki Chutney
Dal	Palak Aloo
Kheer	Rasgullah

Typical Evening Meals

Matar Pulao	Pulao Rice
Karahi Chicken	Chicken Curry
Bindi ki Sabzi	Pooris
Paratha	Milli Sabzi
Gulab Jamun	Sooji Halwa
Raita	Raita

GLOSSARY

Basmati rice: has a nutty flavor and light aroma to it. Rice is washed thoroughly and soaked for about fifteen minutes before cooking to get the best results.

Cardamoms: There are two types of cardamoms, little green ones and larger black ones. Both of these are used in the curry dishes as well as when preparing rice. The little green cardamoms are also used in desserts. They have a subtle sweet aroma.

Chickpea flour: is called *besan* or gram flour and it is made of chickpeas. A few things are prepared from this flour like pakoras and dahi baras.

Chilies: in different forms are used frequently. Fresh green chilies are used in many dishes, sometimes whole chilies are dipped in gram flour and deep fried. Chili powder is an important ingredient of almost all dishes. Dried whole red chilies are also used frequently in vegetable and some meat dishes.

Chili Blend: is a combination of ancho powder, salt, garlic, paprika, oregano, cumin and coriander. Chili blend is one of the main ingredients in cholay.

Cilantro/Fresh coriander: In Pakistan cilantro is actually called coriander. It is used fresh to garnish most dishes. Fresh cilantro goes bad in a few days, I like to freeze it in the ice cube tray. Just drop a cube when cooking and it works.

Cinnamon: Cinnamon sticks are used with other whole spices in curries and rice. Cinnamon is also used in tea with cloves and small cardamoms, during winter. Just add these whole spices when boiling water for tea, makes good masala tea.

Cloves: are unopened flowers, they come from an evergreen tree. They are used whole in most curries, tea and some desserts. They are also known to be a good remedy for toothache. In olden days, people will bite on a clove to help the pain.

Coriander: is used to thicken the sauce and has a strong flavor as well as lemony aroma. The powder is widely available in most ethnic and gourmet spice stores.

Dal: these are the different types of lentils. They are cooked with some spices on their own or with meat. It is very tasty especially during winter months, creates a hearty meal when served with plain rice.

Garam Masala: this is one of the most important ingredient in Pakistani cooking. Garam masala is a combination of five spices, coriander, cumin, cinnamon, black pepper and cloves. All whole spices are slightly roasted and then grounded to powder form. It is kept in an airtight jar. Good quality garam masala stays potent for many months.

Garlic: usually minced and fried with onions and ginger to make the base of a curry. Fresh chopped garlic is used frequently as well. If fresh garlic is not available, only then is the powdered form used.

Ginger: an essential ingredient which is used with garlic for the curry base. Fresh sliced ginger is also boiled in water for tea, especially during winter times. Powdered form is rarely used in cooking.

Red chilli peppers-whole dried: it is usually added in the hot oil in the initial stages of cooking to release the hot flavor. It can make the curries or vegetables quite spicy.

Nigella seeds: also called black onion seeds, these tiny, angular, deep black seeds have a nutty, peppery flavor. They are used in pastries and some vegetable dishes to add flavor.

Saffron: is extracted from the dried stamens of crocus flowers and it is one of the most expensive spices. Saffron is soaked in a few tablespoons of milk for a couple of hours before using it in rice or curries. It adds a strong aroma to the dishes and is used only for special occasions.

Tamarind: can be bought in a block of pulp. It is soaked in water and boiled to get all the juices. The juice is then mixed with spices to make a sauce/chutney.

Turmeric: is golden yellow in color and has a very strong flavor. It is used in small quantities in vegetable and lentil dishes.

INDEX

INDEX